University of Edinburgh
Faculty of Social Sciences Seminar

The Exploding City
edited by W. D. C. Wright and D. H. Stewart

Edinburgh, at the University Press

© EDINBURGH UNIVERSITY PRESS 1972
22 George Square, Edinburgh

ISBN 0 85224 100 3

North America
Aldine · Atherton Inc.
529 South Wabash Avenue, Chicago

Library of Congress
Catalog Card Number 75-106479

Printed in Great Britain by
R. & R. Clark Ltd, Edinburgh

Preface

This book contains a record of both the papers and edited discussions of a Seminar on Urban Growth and the Social Sciences held at the University of Edinburgh from 24th to 26th May 1968. The Seminar was organized by the Faculty of Social Sciences and was the 4th in a series held by the Faculty.

The aim of the Seminar is to provide a forum for the discussion of topics of interest to more than one of the disciplines of the Social Sciences. The subject of Urban Growth seemed to be such a topic. While the papers and discussions range over a variety of aspects and viewpoints, the common concern is with the future wellbeing of our cities and urban life.

The task of organizing the Seminar was shared by a number of colleagues in the Faculty of Social Sciences. The thanks of the participants in the meetings are due to Professor J.N. Wolfe of the Department of Economics whose enthusiasm and energy as the Convener of the Seminars Committee made much possible. Among others to whom a particular debt of gratitude should be acknowledged are Mr R. Bell of the Department of Education and Miss I. Geddie of the Faculty Administrative Office. Thanks are also due to the staff of the Social Sciences Research Centre for their technical assistance recording and transcribing the Seminar.

D.H. Stewart *and* W.D.C. Wright

Contents

Introduction

J.N. WOLFE

The aim of the Edinburgh seminars is to provide a forum for the discussion of topics of interest to more than one of the disciplines of the social sciences. The subject of urban growth seemed to provide an obvious area of concentration both because of its topicality and because of the range of disciplines which could be brought to bear upon it. Economists, Sociologists, Geographers, Planners, Engineers, Architects and Students of Politics could all contribute. The present volume provides an almost unique example of study of this topic from such a variety of viewpoints.

It is of interest to ask which of these disciplines is in fact a social science proper. Certainly economics and sociology would make that claim. Geography and Planning would perhaps regard themselves as already interdisciplinary. Architecture is perhaps part art, part science. As for Politics, views here will differ, but I should myself have regarded Politics as more a social study than a social science.

Yet in spite of the apparent contradictions of putting together natural science, social science, art, social study and interdisciplinary pursuits, there is in practice very little appearance of overlap in the contributions of the various subjects. Indeed what is more striking is the extent to which the contribution of the practitioners of the 'interdisciplinary' subjects like Geography and Planning seemed to possess distinct characteristics of their own, and to have only a limited common ground with the disciplines which they claim to encompass and utilize. I conclude indeed that in spite of popular fiction the subjects of Planning and Geography and Architecture and perhaps even Politics are as much independent social sciences as are Economics and Sociology.

As my defence for this heretical view I would posit a definition of a social science as a subject practised by a distinct group of professionals having a relatively coherent body of principles and a common language. In my submission it will be found that all of the distinct professions represented at this conference qualified according to this definition. While Sociologists, Geographers and Planners might differ among themselves there was no doubt that they had much more in common in approach and language with other members of their profession than with members of any other profession. Surprisingly enough the greatest common ground between the disciplines in terms of approach if not language seemed to be between the engineers and the economists. I leave it to the readers to confirm or deny this observation, and, if the former, to speculate on why this should have been so.

The seminar seems then to have shown up the differences of approach and attitude among the disciplines represented. To have done this is itself a service in the cause of honesty and self-knowledge, and had the seminar done no more it would have been quite worthwhile. But more was, in my view achieved. The contributed papers were so divergent in approach that they succeeded in irritating the participants, and as with the oyster, the reaction to irritation is often something new and valuable.

This valuable reaction is to be found much more in the discussion than in the papers themselves, and for that reason the editors have taken the somewhat unusual step of providing a very full precis of the discussion. It will in my view prove very rewarding reading to the student of any of the social sciences. At the least it provides an astonishingly frank picture of how the social sciences view one another, as well as the problem of urban growth, in the late 1960s.

I now turn to my own subject of economics and discuss what it ought to – but does not yet – contribute to the study of urban growth.

For the economist the greatest problem of urbanization is the exploration and forecasting of the rate of growth of particular cities, and the occupational character of that growth. On these topics economists have so far little to offer beyond well-informed guesses. Most economists believe that the growth of cities derives from the growth of employment opportunities, and that these are in turn the result of the attraction of large labour markets to the industrialist. But while this general impression may be correct, the interesting questions lie in the area of quantification. How important is size of labour force? Does the influence of size grow more than proportionally with size? How significant is distance from the market, and how important is it relative to size? Does the growth of a nearby city act as a stimulus or a depressant upon its neighbours' growth? How important is the possession of so-called growth industries in determining the pattern of growth of cities? And how important is distance from a seaport or major airport?

All of these questions clearly need answering if we are to forecast the growth of cities or the needs for industrial land in them, or the appropriate expenditure on transport facilities to them. And yet we are only now beginning to discover the answers to these questions.

Another question of great importance is the relative size of the tertiary or service sector in the economy of the city. This is of great importance, for planning for it determines the income distribution of the population, their educational needs, and the sort of housing and recreation they expect. If the proportion of the service sector were constant, over time the problem might be insignificant. In fact however the tendencies for cities to retain a definite pattern of secondary and tertiary occupation is not particularly marked.

It remains to be demonstrated that the analytical study of these problems by means of econometric models will produce better prediction than simple extrapolations. Yet even if this should not prove to be the case a good deal will have been learned about the role played by manufacturing and service industry in stimulating the growth of cities, and the importance to be attached to the apparently impending shortage of mobile manufacturing jobs in the last quarter of the century.

There are many fascinating problems to be explored in the field of the economics of urban growth, but perhaps enough has been said to give the reader an idea of the way in which they may be tackled and of their importance for policy.

Essentially the problem is to find quantitative answers to quantitative problems. I hope I will be forgiven if I betray the characteristic prejudice of the economist by saying that it is the movement of the other disciplines of the social sciences in the direction of quantitative results which seems to me to offer the greatest prospect for the development of really useful interdisciplinary contact.

Part One . Sociology

Theories of Environmental Planning and the Social Sciences :
A Critical View
P. Ceccarelli, Professor of Architecture, University of Venice

Sociological Aspects of Urban Growth:
Some Problems of Comprehension
Ruth Glass, Director of Research, Centre for Urban Studies
University of London

Discussion :
A. Travis, Professor of Town and Country Planning
Heriot-Watt University
J.C. Spencer, Professor of Social Administration
University of Edinburgh

Theories of Environmental Planning and the Social Sciences. A Critical View

PAOLO CECCARELLI

Nobody would deny that the theory of environmental planning has been undergoing a profound crisis in recent years : and this holds true for all the operative tools of planning as well. However, it cannot be said that much has been done or is being done to get out of this dead-lock. I think this is a most valuable opportunity to make some re-flections on this crisis and to suggest some ideas, in order to solve it. I believe that we all agree that at this point the gap between urban reality as planners see it and the actual reality of cities has become extremely wide : actually, our debate often makes me think of what Galileo had to say of his Ptolemaic opponents:

'Showing a greater fondness for their own opinions than for truth, they sought to deny and disprove the new things which, if they had cared to look for themselves, their own senses would have demon-strated to them.' [1]

Self-criticism is however of little help. I would rather wish to point out some limitations and inconsistencies in the theoretical framework of environmental planning that we might solve by referring to recent advances made by other social sciences. It is my opinion in fact that the greatest shortcomings and the confusion that we witness among planning theorists result from the very nature of the concepts and categories they make use of in the analysis of the environmental systems and processes. This is most evident, I think, in the study of urban growth. Lacking an adequate description and interpretation of the process of development and of organization of the human en-vironment, planners have both made use of inadequate operative tools and dealt with marginal phenomena – at the wrong levels.

I shall therefore consider how theories of environmental planning deal with the process of urban and regional growth, using this subject as an opportunity to touch upon a more general analysis, that involves not just planners and the practice of planning, but other fields as well.

I intend to show, dealing with some well established approaches to planning, that they rest upon inadequate grounds and are therefore unsatisfactory if considered from the viewpoint of a systematic theoretical analysis; at the same time that the efforts that have been made up to now to solve these limitations can not be accepted as satisfactory.

It seems that an approach giving adequate attention to recent progress in general theory on the part of sociology and social anthropology can be of great importance in solving a number of difficulties and problems and this is a welcome opportunity to start an analysis in this direction.

If we assume that the concern of environmental planning is to express the economic and social goals that a society wants to reach in terms of physical environment, there are three basic problems for a theory of planning : (i) to define the nature and the structure of the existing relationships between socio-economic phenomena and environment; (ii) to define a dynamic model of the variations of the environment in relation to the variations in socio-economic structures; (iii) to define how and why changes in these relationships occur.

Innumerable elements furnish us with evidence that specific relationships exist between social and economic phenomena and physical environment [2]. It is not, however, equally clear what the nature of these relationships is. Are they direct and elementary relationships or indirect and complex ? Are they constant, or do they vary in intensity and type in different socio-economic situations, different environments, or in time ? Do they constitute a system regulated by the laws of necessity, or do they have a casual, accidental character ?

Attempts to provide an answer for these questions have followed two principal approaches, both of which fall in a very broad sense under the heading functionalism.

The first and most generally accepted approach, which I shall call 'structure centred', brings to light the existence of a system of functional interrelations between socio-economic structures and organizational patterns of the physical environment. According to this approach, once the elements which constitute the physical environment and the socio-economic functions corresponding to them have been defined it is possible to construct a typology of systems of interrelations, varying in time and space. In fact, the nature of the system is such that : (*a*) each term of a relation can be explained as a function of another – for example, a given organization of the environment is justifiable with respect to a given cultural pattern, and vice versa for every fixed culture it is possible to identify a particular pattern of environment functional to it; (*b*) each part of the system can be explained in terms of the whole system of relationships – for example, the structure of a human settlement with respect to the entire eco-cultural system of a society.

On these assumptions are based most of the theories of human geography and planning, from Patzel to Vidal de la Blache, from Howard to Le Corbusier, and the current planning practice. For these theories the conditions which give rise to a given human settlement are derived from the existence of specific necessities: the necessity of defence and control, the necessity to produce goods for survival, the necessity of exchange, etc.

To meet these necessities man is forced to develop certain techniques. The nature of these techniques characterizes in turn in various ways the elements of the natural environment and determines different types of human settlements (from a primitive level in which the natural environment has a basic influence, to the level of industrial society in which environment is essentially produced by man, 'artificial'). Specific patterns of spatial organization necessarily correspond to given types of culture and given levels of development.

The development of these relationships in time is presented as a sequence of balanced, static systems. As Max Sorre observes:

'Expression dernière du genre de vie, l'habitat est l'instrument de sa stabilisation. Sa fixité est la marque de l'enracinement du groupe humain. Cela est vrai des établissements urbains comme des établissements ruraux. Cependant, sous la pression du progrès des techniques, les coutumes des hommes et leurs pratiques s'altèrent, les genres de vie anciens se dissolvent ou se transforment. Parce qu'il représente quelque chose de stable, de durable, parce qu'il est de sa nature un élément de permanence, l'habitat semble devoir freiner cette évolution des genres de vie, la cristalliser. Il finit tôt ou tard par évoluer lui aussi.' [3]

The application of this theoretical model to the analysis of reality encounters a series of obstacles. Various studies have indicated that a direct association between a given cultural pattern and a specific type of environment is not to be found frequently. For example, primitive societies of different types exist which develop in environments with comparable characteristics (and vice versa, societies structurally similar whose habitats are entirely different). [4] The relationships among the terms of the system become increasingly complex and indirect as a society develops.

There are several reasons why this direct relationship does not occur or is difficult to identify.

1. In the first place the process of development of a society has a cumulative character; therefore the socio-economic structures as well as the environment develop in time an extremely stratified configuration. The system of relationships between the two terms has a unique character because of the intertwining and the superimposition of various influences and effects. [5]

2. Secondly, the environment, even though it does not tend, like the socio-economic structure, to vary through time, is much more resistant to modification and has much greater inertia; as a consequence cultural patterns become considerably out of phase with respect to the structure of the habitat. [6]

3. Finally, a unitary eco-cultural system in equilibrium is identifiable only in primitive and isolated societies, and as soon as this isolation is broken by normal contact with other cultures or by sudden forced introduction of new techniques, institutions, etc. the equilibrium is destroyed and there is no evidence that it tends to recompose itself. [7] As societies become more complex, an artificial environment is substituted for a natural environment and the latter is extremely specialized and in unstable equilibrium. [8] In these circumstances one must take into account a group of different systems, each of which may tend to equilibrium, but is not necessarily in equilibrium with respect to the others.

The basic evidence on which this approach is based – concerning the system of relationships between society and environment – has a substantial limitation : such evidence indicates that a positive *static* correlation exists between socio-economic development and given patterns of human settlement, but it does not suggest that the same kinds and degrees of association will be found whenever the same set of conditions occurs; neither do they specify the dynamics of the relationships between the variables that are associated, for example, between income, industrialization, and urbanization.

A sequence of development can be described as follows: in the first stage the system of relationships is static and in equilibrium, even if it presents a notable variety of patterns. When development occurs, some groups of relationships are disturbed and new partial systems of relationships, in unstable or partial equilibrium, are continually established. Eventually, through subsequent steps, a new ecological and geographic configuration is substituted for the initial one; the term *ad quem* of the process is a state in which the systems of relationships among the various societies and their environment are more alike. The system of relationships in this stage is again balanced.

On the basis of these elements a predicative model is formulated. The pattern of relationship for the first and the last stages of development are easily definable; this is not the case for the intermediate stage. Under these circumstances one can only build a typology of the relationships that can occur in the transitional stage from one situation to another. [9] They are obviously only abstractions or simplifications of a dynamic process of change, in which infinite and complex patterns among the various elements are interwoven, but they can help to identify structural patterns of the environment apt to facilitate and accelerate the process of evolution toward the final stage of development.

The systems of deductions which uncovers a certain association between socio-economic structures and patterns of environment in a sequence of stages of development is thus concluded. It is now possible to define for each stage of development in a society the kind of spatial organization which maximizes the efficiency of the society itself.

An example of this is provided by some established theories about the way changes in the spatial structuring and distribution of human settlements occur in correspondence with different levels of development of a society. For instance, on the basis of Rostow's theory of the stages of economic development in the past decades many scholars have been engaged in elaborating the hypothesis of a parallel path of economic and physical development. Upon further empirical testing these assumptions have however proved simplistic and inadequate to explain most of the patterns of change occurring in developing areas. [10]

As we have seen, the approach which I have been describing is weakest when it is applied to a changing situation. It is adequate only to describe a static system of relations. Further, by its very nature, it is centred more on the manner in which certain relationships are shaped, than on why they come to be that way.

When one analyses a system which is in transformation, defining the causes of certain processes and of certain trends become indispensable. As has been observed: 'If an institution is changing, one can hardly avoid asking why it is changing in one direction rather than another.' [11] But to this question the 'structure centre' approach is not able to supply a satisfactory answer. Because the emphasis has been placed on the system and on the way events within it are inter-related, the aspects of continuity in a system of relations, the results of certain given variations and the more immediate cause-effect connections are accentuated. This theory is not in a position to predict which may be the spatial counterparts of planned innovations in the socio-economic structure and tends to minimize the importance of every case of non-coincidence or complex relationship between phenomena.

A second point concerns the cumulative character of the process of development. As has been said:

'Few cultural landscapes are entirely products of the work of contemporary communities. The evolution of a landscape is a gradual and cumulative process – it has history. The stages in that history have meaning for the present landscape as well as for those of the past. Moreover, the present cultural landscapes of the world reflect not only local evolutions but also a multitude of influences carried by migration, diffusion, commerce, and exchange. Behind most culture areas of today lies a long succession of different cultures and cultural developments. Culture history, accordingly, must enter strongly into cultural geography.' [12]

Even without attributing to cultural factors a greater importance than that which in fact they have, one certainly cannot leave them out in explaining the complex environmental pattern of a modern society.

A final element embedded in this approach, which I believe has to be clarified, is the resistance of the physical environment to transformations. Various scholars, within the same line of theory, recognize that the ways socio-economic phenomena and environmental organization undergo change are different, and that the timing of the two processes is not the same. [13] This represents an internal limitation of the theory : it means in fact that the time lags and contradictions exist even in the absence of distortion in the society-environment relationships, produced by the cultural stratification of the process of development.

If defining the *genre de vie*, or the culture, of a society which is in the process of change seems to be an abstract goal, it seems even more meaningless to try to define the configuration of the specific pattern of habitat which should correspond to it. This difficulty is particularly evident in the studies of urban growth and diffusion in industrial societies. As has been pointed out:

'The process of urbanization is essentially a process of differentiation among social groups. It is not a transformation of the small community into a large community, nor is it the passage from an old to a new form of social solidarity (Toennies, Durkheim), but it is the rising of a new social entity which is opposed, coexisting, to the proceeding. It is not the expansion of a group, or its disintegration, as Simmel thinks, but the formation of new groups and new types or relations.' [14]

The problem of the relationship between socio-economic phenomena and environment can no longer be understood in terms of static coincidence between cultural patterns and patterns of habitat, but has to be seen in terms of the spatial behaviour of the various groups that make up a given socio-economic system. The coexistence of different conflicting groups is manifested in the way the environment is shaped and controlled, and produces differentiation in the structure of the habitat, disequilibrium among socio-economic structures, etc. We have here the approach that has been called 'behavioural'. [15]

In this case the problem is not how to characterize a given eco-cultural system, but rather to explain why each unit tends to behave in space in a certain way and therefore, interacting with other units, why it generates certain environmental patterns.

While there are few attempts in this direction available in the field of urban theory, several ecological, geographic and economic studies illustrate this type of approach. [16] According to them the population in each habitat organizes specific activities in order to survive. The organization of these activities leads to a distribution in space : the units tend to arrange themselves according to the principle of minimum cost and maximum accessibility.

If in a given habitat, the initial balance between resources and population is altered, competition among individuals increases and they are forced to specialize in order to survive. Specialization allows them to escape partially from the dominant law of competition : the various units are not solely in conflict, but can integrate and help each other. Under such circumstances, the internal mechanism of space distribution remains regulated by a single principle, the economic one; but the ecological structure of the settlements is determined in terms intertwined in specific ways and presents a great variety of combinations.

We can consider the hypothesis that a socio-economic system is composed of units having different levels of ecological dominance and that the ecological structure of the system is characterized by the behaviour of the units occupying the top positions. If this is the case, we can assume the entire spatial structure to be adequate to the requirements of a given socio-economic organization, when the elements of the environment that are directly associated with the behaviour of the dominant units are adequate to the functional requirements of these units. In other words, one has only to adjust those elements of the environment that are necessary to the functioning of the ecologically dominant units in order to adjust the entire system. The impact of such elements upon the entire spatial system, within the context of a specific society, would be such as to represent a new frame of reference for all the remaining elements of the environment. It has been shown, moreover, that the process of development of the environment is characterized by crucial periods in which major innovations are introduced or basic changes occur. [17] It is therefore necessary to analyse the behaviour of the units that are ecologically dominant, particularly at these critical periods, in order to understand the terms of the relationship society-environment. At this point another hypothesis may be introduced; at any given time two elements of disequilibrium or tension can be identified in this relationship. First, the adjustment of the environment to a socio-economic system takes place only through the adjustment of some of its elements to the ecologically dominant units; it follows that when the correspondence among these terms goes below certain levels – e.g., when ecological units with entirely new environmental requirements emerge – a critical period should start. Secondly, since the spatial system is only a static combination of the requirements of specific ecological units at a given time, and since these requirements may change in time, the spatial system should show a decreasing degree of coincidence with the requirements of the units that had originally determined it. Again, under these circumstances a critical period should take place, and a period of innovation should begin.

These hypotheses could explain why advanced socio-economic functions may develop within an environment that as a whole appears to be 'backward', and vice versa. If we assume that, at each step, the process of adjustment of the environment to socio-economic structures is incomplete, related to the specific requirements of particular ecologic units – which belong to given social groups – at any given time, the reason for the stratification and lags would seem to be clarified. Alterations in the system of relationships between society and environmental ways concern a limited number of elements; therefore, the ecological units of the non-dominant groups may either go on using surviving traditional patterns, or adjust to the kind of environment that is forced upon them. Moreover, development proceeds by summation of static spatial patterns, reflecting the functional requirements of the units that are ecologically dominant at any given time. The lack of coincidence in time among terms of the relation is then an intrinsic characteristic of the very process of development.

In many countries modern economic development has produced, and still produces, a system of 'modern' physical elements, that have been superimposed on the complex pre-existing environmental system, that had been shaped through previous epochs, leaving it generally unchanged. The system of settlements, the 'cultural landscapes', etc., have not been modified *in toto*; only some of their elements have been modified, and some new elements have been added. Actually, however, the new system needs only these few crucial elements in order to function. The remainder of the spatial structure is neutral, or in any case non-functional; it may therefore remain unchanged, degenerate or evolve according to its requirements : the degree of freedom is given by the efficiency of the dominant units.

The geography of European industrial societies provides an example of this process. A number of innovations were introduced into the physical structure of the pre-industrial city without destroying it, nor indeed altering it thoroughly according to the new system of spatial relationships. With further changes in the organization of industrial societies, with the increase of service activities, and so on, another system of spatial relationships has been superimposed on the nineteenth-century ones, again without either destroying them or altering them radically. The patterns of development of advanced countries are far from presenting homogeneous and balanced characteristics, and the overlapping and coexistence of the attributes of the pre-industrial society with those of the further phases of evolution is a common phenomenon, which has a significant impact upon the process of development and makes it hard to define.

This is particularly evident in Western Europe, in spite of the long modern history of the various countries; but it is also a relevant characteristic of new socio-economic systems, well advanced in the experience of modernization, such as the US, Canada, or the white societies of Oceania. All advanced societies still present stratified configurations : traditional structures still exist in a new context, often influencing the characteristics of development, and innovations are usually directly conditioned by the surviving elements. This situation may well not be solved at all for a relatively long period of time, or it may even magnify differences in patterns of development.

The same phenomena can be seen in the patterns of settlement of the developing societies. In these it is easy to identify perfectly heterogeneous cultural clusters, connected to a network of modern elements that have been superimposed, in such a way that the entire system functions according to the requirements of the changing socio-economic structure. On the other hand, a model of an 'advanced' spatial organization may be imposed upon a backward society, only partially upsetting the traditional social and economic structures.

Several problems arise at this point; I will point out those which seem to be most important.

The most recent developments of the 'behavioural' approach have underlined the fact that the structure of the ecological relationships cannot be defined entirely apart from a context of culture and values. The economic principle, for example, appears to explain adequately the ecological structure of human settlements in modern industrial societies, but it does not provide a satisfactory explanation of the ecological interaction taking place in contexts of different cultures and values, as various ecological cross-cultural studies have shown. [18]

A further problem arises in considering the units of behaviour. If the structure and the characteristics of the physical environment are examined in the light of the behaviour in space of given socio-economic units, and if we must take account of the historical and cultural context in which the ecological process occurs, it appears necessary to define which are the significant social and economic units within every social system. The significant 'ecological units' and their spatial behaviour are clearly different within a tribal society from those within an industrial society; we can further hypothesize that in every society fixed 'dominant' groups exist which characterize, by the behaviour of their units, and their system of inter-relations, the structure of the environment. [19]

The distribution in space of human settlements and activities cannot therefore be understood without taking into account the structuring of each society in different groups, without considering the conflicts which can arise among the behaviours of competitive groups. This necessity, as I have indicated above, is for example evident when one analyses the ecology of the settlement of some traditional societies in transformation. The competition, and the coexistence, of primitive socio-economic structures and of new structures appears under extreme conditions and constitutes the most direct consistent guideline in interpreting the extremely contrasting ecological patterns, and consequently, the structure of physical development.

This approach seems more adequate for pointing out causes of given relationships between socio-economic structures and environment; moreover, it allows us to draw a dynamic picture of these relationships. It must, however, be placed in a specific historical and cultural context and this causes new problems and reintroduces old elements of weakness.

The character of the human settlement in the industrial regions of western Europe cannot be understood without taking into account the structure of the capitalist society of the nineteenth century, the conflicts between city and country, the alliance between the urban bourgeoisie and the landowners. Similarly, the human geography of the colonial countries cannot be analysed apart from the conflicts between traditional societies and the rationale of colonial policies.

Moreover we must recognize that environmental factors do not have the same importance in all groups, that they do not all compete for the same type of spatial structure. For some of these groups, in certain types of social organization, the 'control of space' factor can be irrelevant or non existent. They may utilize an already constructed environment without altering it or adjust without serious strains to an environment imposed upon them by other groups. For other groups, however, or for the same ones in a different socio-economic context, the issue of the control of space can be one of the bases for survival or one of the reasons for dominance.

However, the significant sociological and economic units whose spatial behaviour we must study should be specified. The concept of 'ecological unit' is ambiguous. In advanced societies, are, for instance, private entrepreneurs, public authorities, the family ecological units? In colonial countries, the colonial administration, foreign enterprises, the clan, the kinship group? On what basis are these units defined and selected?

Also the role of a given unit in shaping the environment, within one society, may be performed in another society by an entirely different ecological unit.

In seeking to formulate a more precise classification and a new typology of the relationships between socio-economic factors and environment, it is easy to slip back into a functional theory as schematic and deterministic as the 'structure centred' one, in which the concept of cultural pattern has been substituted by the concept of ecological unit. The summary relationship : to each given culture corresponds a given habitat, is often merely translated into a summation of sub-relationships, of the following kind : to each of all ecological units corresponds a given habitat. This apparently provides a more articulated picture of the environmental patterns, but actually has the same shortcomings and the same rigidity as the former approach.

I have tried to reappraise briefly the two main theoretical models which are current in the field of planning, analysing their inconsistencies and shortcomings. I am not sure that what I have been saying is sufficiently clear, and I apologise for this, but let me in any case conclude with some statements which may be useful for further discussion.

We may start with a general problem : 'structure centred' approach is the one which has more points in common with the structural-functional theory in sociology and social anthropology, and problems which have emerged in the preceding analysis are the basic problems which the current debate on functionalism has had to deal with. [20] But I would say that the use made in the field of planning of theoretical concepts and models which had been elaborated in different contexts has emphasized latent inconsistencies of the general model.

In other instances we observe arbitrary adjustments, grounded upon superficial analogies from hypotheses drawn from the social sciences. What has resulted is a mechanical and substantially inadequate interpretative system, which accounts for several failures when the system is put to a test.

The question is, however, can we, as of this moment, do without this theoretical system, and substitute it with a viable alternative? I should say no and I have pointed out a number of problems that emerge in the attempts that have been made to elaborate alternatives. I think we are led to conclude that at this time the structural-functional model with all its limitations, cannot be disposed of by the science of environmental planning.

But is this not the same general problem that social theory is facing at this moment? And if we want to solve it, in what direction should we work?

The 'behaviour centred' approach opens up perspectives of further development and the model it presents of the mechanism of environmental development is more articulate. Actually, it explains the process of change *internally*, and allows us to see what the factors are which give rise to it, which is not true of the first approach. And what is more important still, it might change the very meaning of the relationship between the social sciences and planning.

I wish to emphasize this last point, which I think opens up the possibility of a new approach to the whole problem. So far the contributions that the various sciences have been called upon to give to the planning of human settlements have been to support and validate, *from the outside* so to speak, the idea itself and the practical operations of physical planning. Planning as such, however, has been restricted to the physical sphere, the solution to problems of housing, transportation, and organization of space consisting in all cases in changes in the physical structure. In other words the final result of the process – though it did take into account variables to be dealt with in terms of other disciplines – has always had to do with the physical structure, never with the factors that impinge upon it.

Many problems of the development and control of the physical environment might however be approached by instruments other than the traditional physical ones. If we shift our attention to the way individuals and institutions behave in space, rather than limit ourselves to analyzing the effects of such behaviour on the physical structure, many problems which are at present considered as pertinent to environmental planning would become pertinent to social and economic planning.

As a consequence it would become possible either to assign to environmental planning tasks that specifically belong to it and / or to elaborate more effective operational tools for dealing with urban and regional problems.

The confusion between the specific area of interest of environmental planning and the fields of economic and social planning has not only caused negative effects operationally, it has also prevented environmental planners from further developing methods and techniques pertaining to their own field. Not only do the actual boundaries of environmental studies in respect to other social sciences need to be more clearly drawn, but the process of planning itself ought to be substantially rationalized and systematized.

The criteria on which choices are grounded, the elements for testing the congruence between decisions and results, the rules for judging how relevant a phenomenon is, and so on, should be internal to the field of environmental planning in itself, avoiding any reference to 'exogenous' tests derived from socio-economic planning. In a word, environmental planners, should at last begin to 'parler Marivaux, non autour de Marivaux' as Leo Spitzer once remarked referring to linguistics. [21]

I need not say that this way of looking at the relationship between environmental planning and the other social sciences requires further investigation and discussion. What I meant to do in these concluding remarks was to draw from the previous analysis some implications of more general interest.

REFERENCES

1. Galileo Galilei, 'Letter to the Grand Duchess Christina', in *Discoveries and Opinions of Galileo*, Stillman Drake (ed.) (Garden City, N.Y. Doubleday & Co., 1957), p 175.
2. Cf. among others, N. Ginsburg, *Atlas of Economic Development* (Chicago, The University of Chicago Press, 1961); B. J. L. Berry, 'Some Relations of Urbanization and Basic Patterns of Economic Development', in *Urban Systems and Economic Development*, Forrest R. Pitts (ed.) (Eugene, Ore., The School of Public Administration, University of Oregon, 1962); Simon Kuznets, 'Consumption, Industrialization, Urbanization', in *Industrialization and Society*, B. F. Hoselitz and W. E. Moore (eds.) (Paris and the Hague, UNESCO and Mouton, 1963).
3. Max Sorre, *Les Fondements de la Géographie Humaine* (Paris, Colin, 1952), III, p 6.
4. Cf. C. Daryll Forde, *Habitat, Economy and Society : A Geographical Introduction to Ethnology* (New York, E. P. Dutton, 1963).
5. See A. E. Smailes, *The Geography of Towns* (London, Hutchinson, 1953), pp 84–134; also R. McC. Adams, *Land Behind Baghdad, A*

History of Settlement on the Diyah Plains (Chicago, University of
Chicago Press, 1965). For an analysis of the stratification of cultural
patterns of B. Malinowski, *The Dynamics of Culture Change* (New
Haven, Conn., Yale University Press, 1945); also A. L. Kroeber,
Anthropology: Culture Patterns and Processes (New York, Harcourt,
Brace & Co., 1963).

6.   Max Sorre, op. cit., III, pp 23 ff; also A. Demangeon, *Problèmes de
Géographie Humaine* (Paris, Colin, 1952), 4th edition, pp 153 ff.

7.   See for instance, L. Thompson, 'The Relations of Men, Animals
and Plants in an Island Community (Fiji), in *American
Anthropologist*, LI (April–June 1949); E. E. Evans-Pritchard,
*The Nuer, a Description of the Modes of Livelihood and Political
Institutions of a Nilotic People* (Oxford, Oxford University Press,
1963), 6th edition, pp 50 ff; also, R. Redfield, *The Little Community*
(Chicago, The University of Chicago Press, 1960), pp 29 ff.

8.   P. Wagner, *The Human Use of the Earth* (New York, Free Press, 1964),
pp 22–3.

9.   On the possibility of building such a model cf. W. E. Moore, *Social
Change* (Englewood Cliffs, N. J., Prentice-Hall, 1964), 2nd edition
pp 41 ff.

10.   See for instance John Friedmann, *Regional Development Policy. A Case
Study of Venezuela* (Cambridge, Mass., The M.I.T. Press, 1966),
especially chapter I; also Leonard Reissman, *The Urban Process.
Cities in Industrial Societies* (New York, The Free Press, 1964), chapter
VIII. In many of these studies of development, socio-economic
systems have been categorized with reference to some clusters of
attributes. It has been said for instance that an advanced country is
characterized by the existence of a given per capita income level,
a given percentage of the labour force in manufacturing and service
jobs, a given level of urbanization, etc. But one cannot by any
means assume that if a society has some of these attributes, all of
the others will automatically be present.

Kuznets indicates, in this connection, that even though
industrialization and urbanization are generally highly correlated,
from a theoretical standpoint there is no technical connection
between level of industrialization, level of income and level of
urbanization. Even though it is difficult, in practice, to imagine an
industrial society having a loose pattern of settlement, he goes on to
point out that 'this emphasis on the lack of any inevitable
connection between industrialization and urbanization is useful
because it draws attention to the two boundaries at which such a
connection may be weakened' (Simon Kuznets, 'Consumption,
Industrialization and Urbanization', in *Industrialization and Society*,
B. F. Hoselitz and W. E. Moore (eds.) (Paris and the Hague,
UNESCO and Mouton, 1963), p 203.

Thus Kuznets emphasises that there is no necessary automatic
relationship between a given level of economic development and a
particular pattern of urbanization. Theoretically, one could assume
that in two countries having the same conditions of development,
the urban pattern might be substantially different, or vice versa,
that where the environmental pattern shows similar characteristics,
the actual levels of development may be different.

For a broader discussion of Rostow's model of development see
W. W. Rostow (ed.), *The Economics of Take-off into Sustained Growth,*
Proceedings of a Conference Held by the International Economic Association
(New York, St Martin's Press, 1963), cf. specifically the papers of
S. Kuznets, H. J. Habbakuk and Phyllis Deane, and J. Marczewski.

11. George C. Homans, 'Bringing Men Back In', *Amer. Soc. Rev.*,XXIX
     (December 1964), p 810.

12. Philip L. Wagner and Marvin W. Mikesell (eds.), *Readings in Cultural*
     Geography (Chicago, University of Chicago Press, 1962), p 13.

13. Ibid.

14. Alessandro Pizzorno, 'Economic Development and Urbanization',
     in *Transactions of the Fifth World Congress of Sociology*, Washington
     (September 1962), II, p 99.

15. D. L. Foley, 'An approach to Metropolitan Spatial Structure', in
     Explorations into Urban Structure, M. M. Webber and others (Phila-
     delphia, University of Pennsylvania Press, 1964), pp 53–6.

16. See G. A. Theodorson (ed.), *Studies in Human Ecology* (Evanston, Ill.,
     Row, Peterson & Co., 1961); Allan Pred, *Behavior and Location.*
     Foundations for a Geographic and Dynamic Location Theory, Part I (Lund,
     The Royal University of Lund, Department of Geography, 1967);
     also M. M. Webber and others, op. cit.

17. A good example of this is offered by the process of capital formation.
     In order to achieve a given level of growth, or to determine
     'multiplication effects' in the entire economy, or to avoid bottlenecks
     in the process of development, the timing of the formation of
     fixed capital has to be considered, as well as the quality and type
     of required capital. An infrastructure which is unduly large with
     respect to the needs of a specific period, not only implies
     unnecessary expenditures, and is an underutilized asset, but its
     very existence may well hinder the possibility of further
     investments in overhead capital, at the time when they might
     prove – in general socio-economic terms – much more productive
     (see for instance what Gerschenkron has remarked about the
     Italian industrialization of 1896–1908 (Alexander Gerschenkron,
     Economic Backwardness in Historical Perspective (Cambridge, Mass.,
     Harvard University Press, 1962, p 84). On the other hand, unduly
     restricted policies of capital formation may produce effects just as
     negative. Beyond a certain point, it is not enough to allocate a
     constant share of expenditures in order to insure a regular increase
     of fixed capital : it is necessary to concentrate a large share of
     investments in this sector at the right time, if dangerous bottlenecks
     are to be avoided (see on this problem, A. O. Hirschman, *The*
     Strategy of Economic Development (New Haven, Yale, University
     Press, 1958)).

18. A. B. Hollingshead, 'A Re-examination of Ecological Theory',
     in *Sociology and Social Research*, XXXI (January–February 1947),
     W. Firey, *Land Use in Central Boston* (Cambridge, Mass., Harvard
     University Press, 1947), Introduction; also G. A. Theodorson, op. cit.
     For some provocative remarks on ecological theory see also
     Alessandro Pizzorno, Introduction to the Italian translation of
     R. E. Park, E. W. Burgess, R. D. McKenzie, *The City* (Milano,
     Edizioni di Comunità, 1967). An interesting description of

different systems of ecological interaction originated by different
sets of values can be found in Claude Lévi-Strauss, *Anthropologie
Structurale* (Paris, Plon, 1958), pp 148–51, with reference to
Radin's studies on the organization of the Winnebago's settlements.

19. See for instance B. Harris, 'The Uses of Theory in the Simulation
of Urban Phenomena', *AIP Journal*, xxxi (September 1966), pp
269–71; also I.S. Lowry, 'A Short Course in Model Design', in
AIP Journal xxxi (May 1965), p 158. For an evaluation of the
different concept of 'unit' in the analysis of primitive societies of
D.M. Schneider, 'Some muddles in the Models', in *The Relevance
of Models for Social Anthropology*, A.S.A., Monographs 1 (London,
Tavistock Publications, 1965), pp 47 ff.

20. Cf., among others, K. Davis, 'The Myth of Functional Analysis as
a Special Method in Sociology and Social Anthropology, in *Amer. Soc.
Rev.*, xxiv (1959); G.C. Homans, op. cit.; also W.E. Moore,
Social Change (Englewood Cliffs, N.J., Prentice-Hall, 1964),
2nd edition.

21. L. Spitzer, 'A propos de la Vie de Marianne' (Lettre à M. Georges
Poulet), in *The Romantic Review*, xliv (1953),p 102.

Sociological Aspects of Urban Growth.
Some Problems of Comprehension

RUTH GLASS

The topic set – sociological aspects of urban growth – is a large one; and the time allotted to it is short. The subject is vast, not least because seen in international perspective it is at present relevant primarily to developing countries. It is they which are now in the phases of urban growth – phases which have, strictly speaking, been largely completed in the industrialized countries of the world. So perhaps you will allow me to use this half-hour for airing some of the perplexities which arise, inevitably, in reviewing the subject, though these are of course well known, and reflected in the literature of urban studies.

At every stage in such a review, we come up against barriers to comprehension. There are exceptional difficulties in 'taking in' the phenomena of urban growth in developing countries; in understanding their implications; in making generalizations; and so in drawing policy conclusions. And there are many obvious reasons for such difficulties. To mention a few, though not in order of priority.

For instance : the problem of comprehension is highlighted, presumably to many of us, whenever we are confronted with one of the actual scenes of urban existence and change in a 'developing' country – a scene so manifold, so crowded, so amazingly rich in its visual impact. How can one retain the 'integrity' of the moment? It does not seem much of a problem when we go through familiar places in Edinburgh or London, in Liverpool or Norwich. In such circumstances, all observations are in a sense already preclassified. But it is a very different matter when we walk through a bustee in Calcutta; a bazaar in Old Delhi; a tenement street in Singapore; a strangers' colony in Kumasi. We are then newcomers with wide open eyes, aware of how little we can see, and yet wanting to see everything at once. And there is usually a moment when one can recognize (or believes one can recognize) both the whole and the parts; the mass and the individuals; the concrete scene and its more abstract meaning. But a second later, the picture has already slipped away; it has become blurred, broken up; only some segments are remembered. So we shall never know how much of it we have missed; and to what extent it has become distorted. Even if our minds were ciné cameras, and all the reels could be played back, the frustration arising from the inability to encapsule the experience would still remain.

Of course, this is a perennial problem of human perception, important in all processes of learning. How can one record, and how can one convey, the total reality? In social investigations all sorts of attempts have been made to deal with it – from Mayhew to Oscar Lewis – some more plausibly than others. But still the difficulty of seeing the wood for the trees, or the trees for the wood, is an acute one, especially in a field, such as that of urban development, to which observation is guided to preconceived notions, and by rather vague criteria of selection.

This brings me to another sphere of comprehension, more humdrum and more technical – the kind of complications which are largely produced by the tools of analysis which we use. There are considerable difficulties in assessing rates, and in comparing phenomena, of urban growth – difficulties which should not be belittled, and which take up a lot of time and effort. Both the data on which such assessments are based, and their categorization, are generally rather poor; the definitions are ambiguous; the area boundaries tend to be arbitrary.

For example: what is 'urban'? We all know that there are several definitions – in terms of physical, administrative, occupational or cultural criteria; in terms of the population size or institutional equipment of a settlement. These criteria are used singly or in varying combinations in different censuses; and of course the results thus obtained are not necessarily compatible or comparable.[1] Moreover, a hierarchy of different ranks, or classes, of urban areas is built up: towns, cities, conurbations, metropolitan areas or regions. With each step in the categorization, the distinctions become more arbitrary; more equivocal; more deceptively precise.[2] The impression is created, however unjustifiably, that like has been grouped with like. But is there a common urban species – a family of towns and cities to which such disparate places as Edinburgh and Ibadan, Pittsburgh and Perugia, Cheltenham and Cochin belong?

Questions of this kind might be dismissed as pedantic academic exercises but for the fact that they also have direct practical implications. For the purpose of tracing trends in any one country, such as Britain, it does not matter much how 'urban' places are defined, provided that the definition is reasonably consistent and comparable over time.[3] But as soon as we turn to international comparisons, the ambiguities in data collection and classification become very important, the more so if they create a pretension of accuracy as they tend to do. When a parade of statistics looks so solid, it is easy to forget that it is nothing of the kind. On the other hand, there is also inevitably an inclination to utilize their weakness; to reject data which do not readily conform to prejudices.

This inclination is particularly strong in the field of urban affairs, which is still dominated by all sorts of romantic and apocalyptic notions. Hence the frequent Cassandra cries about the grim prospects of urbanization in the world today – though in fact the data indicate that by and large the rate of urbanization, as distinct from urban growth, is not dramatically high. Nowadays, urbanization proceeds apparently more slowly in most developing countries of Asia, Africa and Latin America than it did in Europe and North America in earlier periods.

While the distinction between urban growth and urbanization is an elementary one, essential for policy reasons, it is often ignored. In technical parlance, 'urban growth' is the absolute increase of the urban population, at the same or similar rate as that of the total population. By contrast, 'urbanization' is the proportionate increase in the urban population – a greater increase than that of the total population of a given country or region over a period of time. This can occur either because there is a higher natural increase of the urban than of the rural population; or because of a net influx from rural to urban areas; or because rural areas are reclassified in the urban column : or because of a combination of these various factors.[4]

Again, one also speaks of urban growth, more vaguely, when there is an expansion of urban areas, though this need not be, and is indeed often not, matched by an increase in the population living in such areas. It is usually brought about by a shift to suburban territory; and so by the 'fanning out' of interrelated residential and non-residential land-uses. This process – often accompanied by a general blurring of rural – urban distinctions in occupational and cultural terms – can best be described as 'urban diffusion'. It is now predominant in industrialized countries; and it also occurs already, in conjunction with urbanization and urban population growth, in many developing countries.[5]

It is clearly important to disentangle these phenomena since they have different causes and consequences. Wherever urban growth rather than urbanization is the main trend, as it seems to be at present in many developing countries of the world, the antidote – if it be needed – has to be found primarily in general population policies, in a reduction in the rate of population increase, rather than in specific urban policies.[6] Moreover, in such circumstances the prospects or the rural economy have to be carefully watched since further pressure might well bring about an increase in rural – urban migration, and thus in fact 'urbanization' on top of 'urban growth'.

Though these trends can be observed in broad terms, it is much more difficult to obtain fairly precise unequivocal comparisons of the rates of urban growth or urbanization in different countries. Quite apart from the difficulties arising through urban – rural differentials in the enumeration of the population, and in the registration of births and deaths, there is the further complication (which has been mentioned already) that 'urban' areas and their population can be variously defined. And the conclusions differ according to the scheme of categorization adopted. (For instance : the proportion of the *total* urban population is higher in South-East Europe than in North Africa, but the proportion of the population in large cities, with 100,000 people or more, is the same in both these regions. Thus using one yardstick, one might say that South-East Europe is more urbanized than North Africa; using another, one would conclude that this is not so.[7]

The consequent uncertainties, however, are less embarrassing than the fact that they tend to be brushed aside. A flimsy, primitive foundation of data or pseudo-data is often used to build an elaborate, apparently sophisticated superstructure of appraisal. Is there too much or too little urbanization in some areas of the world? Is it sufficiently matched by industrialization? How can we judge when the questions themselves are rather crude; and when the evidence, moreover, consists of tentative figures relating to ambiguous socio-geographical categories, allied with similar data relating to even more questionable categories of economic activity?[8] Nevertheless, one hears weighty pronouncements about 'over-urbanization' and 'under-urbanization', 'parasitic' and 'generative' urbanization, and other neat dichotomies of this kind. While such models have their uses in pointing to major aspects of development, their empirical basis is still rather slight.

So altogether, when we consider comparative aspects of urban growth, we find a scarcity of data and a surfeit of rather shaky generalizations. Why is this so?

Quite apart from the obvious practical difficulties of data collection, there are some crucial conceptual problems, which in turn impede, and also overcomplicate, empirical work.

The main trouble is that 'we' – the current observers here and elsewhere – are hardly as yet equipped to comprehend the unprecedented complexity, the sheer novelty of contemporary manifestations of development, including those of urban growth. We are conditioned to think in terms of more straightforward development (or of the images of development as they have been passed on); in terms of simpler societies with more clear-cut patterns of stratification.[9] We think in terms of periods when it was possible to impose positive value systems, without much scepticism or resistance. But none of this is applicable any longer.

Most developing countries now have multiple denominators of social stratification – caste, tribalism, ethnic and linguistic grouping, usually intertwined with an emerging class structure. Most of these countries have both neo-colonial and anti-colonial elites : there are people who have maintained, or acquired, the old status symbols and ideology; there are those who have found their status in the struggle for independence. Often the same people have done both, and themselves represent the contradictions. Moreover, different configurations of status systems are found side by side – not least because the conditions and outlook of different periods coexist, often in potential or acute tension, to an extent which has never been experienced before. All these countries have 'backward' classes, or 'inferior' minorities, next to, and usually dominated by, highly advanced groups. And this kind of socio-historical stratification is visible especially in many of the cities, which consist of an agglomeration of societies. In many respects, if not in most, they are simply not comparable to Western cities in the stages of rapid urbanization.[10]

Similarly, old problems of poverty and new problems of comparative prosperity coexist, and intensify each other. The old urban congestion is getting worse, and is already complicated by new hordes of private motorists. Quite often the number of private cars multiplies at a much more rapid rate than the number of seats on trams or buses. Various phases of development – urban growth and urban diffusion – occur simultaneously, and interfere with each other. Suburban sprawl of the most wasteful kind upsets long-term plans for a systematic redistribution of increasingly competitive urban land-uses. The rows of middle-class villas stretch out while the shanty towns become denser; and there are still hardly any water taps or latrines. The poor are left in, or even pushed into, marginal locations, with only precarious access to the urban labour market. Exercises in civic design, derived from some Western textbook on the 'city beautiful' – ornamental additions to a few privileged public places – are well in advance of the most elementary schemes for the alleviation of urban squalor.

Of course, for better and for worse, in the conduct and aspirations of developing countries, international linkages are now far more evident than they were for the industrialized nations in their previous periods of development. The models have become both less and more hypothetical. The people of Asia, Africa and Latin America do not need to invent their utopias; they see them in this world, at the present

time, sometimes just around the corner. And since their institutions
and values are indeed multilateral, exceptional efforts have to be made
to achieve some coherence.

There are many conflicting norms. And so it has become more
difficult than ever before to find criteria of analysis and evaluation;
to establish priorities, or even systematic rules of observation. What
is one to do when economic 'development' is evidently so ambivalent
a process, with so many contradictory implications? It might well
accentuate inequalities, and sharpen social divisions – with the result
that the newly prosperous elites become increasingly isolationist, and
increasingly autocratic in their behaviour to other groups. So the process can produce disintegration as well as integration; it can retard
as well as advance the understanding of the social universe; and
indeed development in every sense of the term.[11] Moreover, in the
short run, too, there are always two sides of the coin. Labour-
intensive employment discourages an increase in productivity. A
spread of education often promotes frustration – the emergence of a
new group of unemployed white-collar workers. Essential public
health measures are bound to extend life expectation, to reduce
mortality, in advance of a compensating reduction in fertility; and so
to complicate the problems of population growth.

No doubt, the risks have to be taken. It is well worth while to
pay the price. Even so, it is hardly surprising that in the face of so
much complexity, observers or participant-observers are quite often
tempted to take the easy way out. They can either profess value
neutrality – and this is usually done by engaging in crude empiricism
and an oversimplified taxonomy.[12]

The still fashionable theme of analysis – 'modern' versus 'traditional' groups and institutions – is an example of the latter approach.
It seems to be so profitable because it is value-loaded : 'modern' is
usually regarded as synonymous with 'good' (or better); and traditional with 'bad' (or worse). In reality, of course, things are not quite
so simple. One of the outstanding aspects of contemporary developing societies is the increasing difficulty in distinguishing clearly
between 'traditional' and 'modern' features. They merge; they reinforce each other. 'Modernization' accentuates 'traditional' conservative ideas or institutions; and vice versa. (For instance : the
traditional elites are strengthened because they undertake modern
entrepreneurial functions; new political parties reflect old caste or
tribal alignments; trade unions or other modern organizations grow
just because they are opposed to innovation, not least to the introduction of modern technology.)

So we need to look again. And most of all, we cannot help being concerned with the constant dilemma, a very real one, which is at the basis of all our trials and errors in the perception of contemporary social changes, in general, and of urban growth, in particular. It is the old problem of establishing valid generalizations in a new form. There is the dilemma : how to avoid cultural ethnocentricity without resorting to cultural relativism in a rather defeatist manner. On the one hand, it makes no sense merely to borrow extraneous ideas or analogies for the analysis of current phenomena of development. On the other hand, it is hardly possible to make any progress, intellectual or practical, on the assumption that every situation is *sui generis*.

Put in these general terms, the problem is rather baffling. In practice, in relation to concrete aspects of urban development, it is more manageable. Anyhow, there is one conventional idea at least which need certainly not be rejected out of hand – the hope that urban growth itself, now as in the past, will be a learning process. So while I started with a recital of perplexities, I have no hesitation in concluding on a tone of optimism.

NOTES

1. For instance : both Britain and the United States are even more highly urbanized in terms of cultural or occupational criteria (such as the proportion of the labour force in non-agricultural occupations) than in terms of the proportion of the population living in areas, classified as urban. In most developing countries the position is the reverse : there is more urbanization in terms of administrative than of occupational criteria.
2. While a demarcation of urban areas in terms of their administrative status (such as urban districts, boroughs and county boroughs in this country) has some limitations – it does not necessarily include the urban hinterland – it is at least based on a clear-cut definition of local government boundaries. But the construction of larger aggregates (metropolitan areas or regions) for statistical purposes can be, and usually is, a much more ambiguous and indeed controversial matter. This was illustrated, for example, when the area of Greater London was defined by statute in 1963. It could well be argued that this definition was already out-of-date by that time – that the 'real' London was greater still.
3. However, this is not invariably so. In some circumstances – for instance, in a vast country such as India, with considerable regional variations in settlement patterns – it is much more difficult to find a definition of 'urban' places which is generally applicable and truly comparative.

4. In other words, there can be urban growth without urbanization.
   In principle, there can also be urbanization without urban growth.
   This would happen when the total population of a country
   declines, but the urban population remains stationary or declines
   at a slower rate.

5. This trend of 'urban diffusion' has been visible in Britain since the
   beginning of the century. It was admirably projected by H. G.
   Wells in a chapter on 'the probable diffusion of great cities' in his
   book *Anticipations*, first published in 1900. (The full title of the
   book was 'Anticipations of the reduction of mechanical and
   scientific progress upon human life and thought'.) In this country,
   the trend has been further accelerated in the last two decades.
   For instance: all conurbation centres with the exception of
   Leeds – not only London (the old County) – have shown a
   population decline between 1951 and 1961. And this decline has
   been even more marked from 1961 to 1966. During that period
   there has been an exodus not only from the 'parent' cities (the
   conurbation centres), but also from the outer areas of the
   conurbations.

6. Though the main trends are clear, the basic data are too scarce or
   imprecise to make hard and fast statements. (Hence the proviso – 'it
   seems to be so' – in referring to such a trend.) However, there is
   little doubt that the *natural increase* of the urban population, rather
   than migration, is the major element in urban growth in many
   countries. For instance : it has been estimated that natural increase
   accounts for 58 per cent of the population growth in towns (in
   those with 20,000 or more people) in Mexico; for 66 per cent in
   Venezuela; for 70 per cent in Chile. In many areas of Asia these
   proportions would be higher still. (See, e.g., Edourdo E. Arriaga,
   'Components of City growth in selected Latin American countries',
   Milbank Memorial Fund Quarterly, April 1968).

7. Since the definitions of 'urban' places, and thus of the *total* urban
   population, are so variable, and often non-comparable, in different
   censuses, a better comparison is usually obtained by using the
   yardstick of the population in larger towns (in or beyond the
   20,000 or 100,000 size groups). But this, too, has snags – if one
   compares, for example, Ceylon and India – since the size, incidence
   and importance of cities is of course relative to the total population
   size of the country in which they exist.

8. On the whole, the occupational and industrial categories used are
   far too general and too vague to permit a genuine comparative
   assessment of the economic basis of urban areas in different
   countries. For instance : all sorts of diverse groups – from women
   who sell a few carrots at a street corner to cashiers in a supermarket
   – are included under the heading of workers in the 'tertiary sector',
   or even in the more specific category of retail trade. Such simple
   classifications are misleading, quite apart from the fact that they
   cannot take account of variations in employment and remuneration
   (underemployment and casual employment; payment in cash or in
   kind). Similarly, the apparently most clear-cut distinctions – such as
   that between 'urban' and 'rural' occupations – are not necessarily
   the most meaningful ones. Is highly organized work in a sugar

factory or on a factory farm really more 'rural' than that done by a lone carpenter or seamstress in the doorway of a back alley?

9. It is certainly not only the 'outsiders', people in industrialized countries, who think in these terms. The views of 'opinion leaders', and especially of social scientists, in developing countries are still largely conditioned by ideas borrowed from Western societies.

10. The colonial background of many of these cities gives them distinct characteristics. Many of them, too, show a far more obvious and more persistent rural–urban mixture than was seen elsewhere in previous periods – although they frequently expand more through indigenous natural increase than through migration. Thus the much maligned shanty towns, for example, quite often look like transplanted villages – like places which have the worst of both worlds. Many of them have village-type housing. But it has become stifling, walled-in, impoverished, so to speak, in the over-crowded urban location, where the lack of basic services, of water and sanitation, is inescapable. Even so, of course, this quasi-rural look can be deceptive. The people of the shanty towns, too, often have already quite a substantial economic base in the city. Again, established communities, together with recent arrivals belonging to kindred groups, frequently form distinct colonies. There is a good deal of segregation; and not necessarily a classic 'melting pot' situation.

11. Such sharpening of social divisions, and the consequent increasing social segregation, is of course one of the most important elements in the understanding, or rather in the misunderstanding, of actual developments. It affects comprehension, directly and indirectly, at every level, including the exercises of social scientists. The case of the shanty towns, bustees, barrios, favelas, which has already been mentioned, is a striking example. They are generally regarded as the villains of the piece, and as the 'fifth column' of urbaniza-tion, by conservatives and radicals alike. Their neglect is tolerated or even justified; they remain segregated; and so they are not clearly recognized at all. Instead of considering the great variety in their conditions and social organization, they are pictured in terms of stereotypes. But in fact the social fabric of these places is often far more substantial than their artifacts. The people of the shanty towns are certainly not all refugees from the countryside; new-comers; marginal men. Many of them have already found a place in the urban economy.

12. Though there is a considerable volume of empirical work relating to urban growth in developing countries, it has tended to be rather erratic so far. By and large it consists either of 'macro-statistics', mainly fairly raw data, unaccompanied by analysis, or of purely descriptive 'microstudies' of specific areas or groups. Only rarely are the statistics and the descriptions 'married' to one another – that is, only rarely are the descriptions focussed on systematically selected parts of a statistically defined universe. (However, there are exceptions, especially in the literature on Latin America.)

Discussion

A. TRAVIS

Professor Ceccarelli has accused those who have been concerned with sorting out the physical shell, of a lack of understanding of the relationships between the *physical* environment and the *social* environment. The situation has become polarized since the turn of the century, when there was very much of a working interchange between them. They have become separated into different channels; the sociologist has become (possibly) more concerned with a deeper understanding of social situations, whilst the planner and the others, like social administrators, and political decision-makers, have become concerned with attempts at controlling the nature of change of our physical surroundings. They have tended to make many over-simple assumptions about the nature of the relationship between the physical and the social environments. This is the myth which has been at the basis of a hundred years of development in public health and in planning. The essential dogma is one of *environmental determinism*; if the physical environment is very bad, people are unhappy, so the question is turned in on itself. You create a good physical shell and this will make people happy. This point recurs very effectively in Dr Ceccarelli's paper, particularly at the beginning.

I would like to challenge his assumption that the concern of physical planning is to express the economic and social goals. I think there has been gross confusion within these groups of decision-makers as to the real nature of the social and economic situations. The general point can perhaps be made best by taking the extreme example. Two cases that many of us have been thinking about and talking about in the last year or so are extreme cases of failure, like the Stanstead Airport, and the Edinburgh ring-road. Here we have the rare example of groups which are affected by decisions that they have not had an effective part in making, but which have the ability and the power to communicate a legitimate response view to others. Dr Ceccarelli sees this situation as being one, internationally, of crisis. I would support this proposition because it seems that only in odd examples in the United States are we attempting to go back to fundamentals in such things as understanding the nature of objectives and values.

Perhaps we will come to the point where we begin to accept the heterogeneous nature of social environments. I think that this immediately rules out the idea of trying to plan on the basis of laying down 'universal' rules or 'universal' standards which may apply to the nation or even to a city; it leads to the view that one may have to devise and evolve standards which are particular to certain situations. This perhaps is a very radical view, but how in fact can we go back towards a synthesized situation? A social survey in 1945/46 that was part of the Middlesbrough Plan is perhaps symptomatic of the problem. In studying the city, a considerable amount of time and attention was given to understanding the nature of the physical animal in relation to the social structure. Yet when one comes round to the decision-making process, we are unable satisfactorily to resolve those questions in terms of the ability of the physical shell to answer a new situation, in terms of a new shell for existing people.

As Dr Ceccarelli has implied there must also be a questioning once again of the whole philosophical basis of action; the planners are not animals in isolation, they are supposedly interpreters on behalf of society.

J. C. SPENCER

Dr Ceccarelli raised some of the very important problems of collaboration between the social sciences and the planner, and in particular the value of structural models. Looking back from the past history of the contribution of social science concepts to planning, one would be bound to emphasize the persistence of what might be called sociological myths in the planning field. In the early days, the rather rudimentary theories concerning neighbourhood units, as well as some of the views on social mixing, are illustrations of this point. It is clearly Dr Ceccarelli's intention to try and facilitate the evolution of a more scientific basis for the planning in which he is engaged. In doing this, he raised some very interesting points on which I should like him to talk.

In particular he places a great deal of emphasis on an area which assumed great importance in early sociological theory, i.e. the field of ecology. In my own field of criminology, ecology at one time was of central importance to the study of crime, but one might say that this major contribution came to an end with the disappearance of the Chicago School under Burgess and Park. Several times in his paper Dr Ceccarelli talked about the behaviour of what he calls 'ecologically-dominant units', and placed great emphasis on this in the development of the social sciences.

I want first to ask him what he really means by these 'ecologically-dominant units'. He says for example that the behaviour of the ecologically-dominant units have been studied because the adjustment of the environment to the socio-economic system takes place only through the adjustment of some of its elements of these units. Then he argues that the ecological units of the non-dominant groups may continue to follow traditional patterns.

Secondly I want to ask Mrs Glass to pursue the very interesting implications for social policy which follow from her paper. I think that those who are concerned in this field have to be extremely cautious in transferring ideas of social policy developed in Western society, to the very different structure and conditions of the under-developed countries. In the course of her paper Mrs Glass brought out well the problem of contradictions, not only in terms of definitions, but also in terms of the data available, such as occupational structure, and the coexistence of poverty and affluence. It seems to me that one of the difficult questions facing a social scientist before he can give assistance to planners, is the need to be clearer about the implications of contradictions which emerge in studies of under-developed societies, but which an industrialized Western country does not have to face in the same way. For instance Mrs Glass made a point about ethnic enclaves and the way in which these cut across each other.

GENERAL DISCUSSION

Dr Glass. I think that the contradictions which Professor Spencer mentions are really complexities. I did not intend to induct that earlier theories of class or power systems in conflict are obsolete, but they do have to be elaborated. We cannot understand what is going on in Nigeria at the present time simply by using a classical Marxist model.

It still has much to tell us, but we clearly have to become a little bit more versatile.

To take up one other point, Professor Travis referred to some sociological myths in planning. We must realize that they are not in fact sociological myths at all. These were the inferences of people like Patrick Geddes and some of their followers. The real problem is simply this mechanistic idea about the relationship between environment and society, which incidently bedevils a great deal of thought in the developing countries. The idea that the bigger the city the greater the problems and so on is not necessarily the case. This is really the context that has understandably been taken up by the planning profession. Saying that one has to be more versatile, or more realistic, does not mean that one has to make such terribly heavy weather about it. Take for a moment the empirical approach of some of the late nineteenth and early twentieth-century social scientists. If they had been used more in this country we might have been a bit better off. Planners would not have worked on absolutely phoney statistical averages, like the average family size which has made our housing policy in this country so odd. Why should we not simply say that there are certain kinds of human functions in cities which are fairly general. We have to have fairly general space and land use needs that get varied to a certain extent according to diverse patterns.

P. Ceccarelli. Professor Spencer asked what I mean by ecological units. There has been a reappraisal of many of the concepts and the contributions that ecologists give to the study of urban processes, especially after studies in the United States rediscovered the subcultural problems the planners had to deal with in the very large cities.

There are rules of the game that are fixed by groups in the city, which I call 'units'. The units could be big enterprises, or government authorities, having their own rationale. Some of the largest, most important groups connected with the power structure of the city or regions have a rationale in deciding how they want the city or region to develop. Because they have some goals to fulfil, they influence the process of development that they are sponsoring.

For instance I am involved in the plan for the development of a big new car factory around Naples. The problem we have there is that there are many powerful government agencies operating with very different rationalities, and having not very clear goals to meet in developing the region.

We are trying to rationalize the process of development within these varied rules.

These groups were acting with different rules to fulfil different kinds of goals and we are trying to rationalize these goals. What was good for one of the groups was not good for another and of course the winners in some way decided and structured the physical features of that area.

It is the same kind of phenomenon that you have in the developing countries when they want big planning operations to be undertaken. The government may decide to achieve a development objective which it is trying to impose on the local culture. In general, we have this in any kind of city planning process. My point was to see if it was possible to reconnect many of these facts or to alter the position of ecological studies.

P. E. A. Johnson-Marshall. Plans are not made in a vacuum – in most cases it is politicians who make all the decisions and planners only offer advice on physical form for politicians to make the decisions. First of all we need better decision-making by the politicians and a better basis for advice by planners. In this sense the planners need more clear information of social needs. In some cases planners have

In the nineteenth- and early twentieth-century slum clearances, the planners were certainly forced into this kind of thinking. In recent plans however, there has been useful contribution made. It is a question of client – planner collaboration. This needs to be clarified – particularly the client's contribution – before one gets on to the physical models.

J. N. Wolfe. I agree with Mrs Glass that for most of the world the most obvious facet of society is the extent to which it is not unified and how very much the different groups of society do not like each other. Do the planners work on the assumption that they could make antipathetic groups like each other by bringing them close together? Do they believe that they could achieve this or do they just think that this was the way people ought to live, irrespective of whether or not they live in harmony when they are brought together? Whether it is the planner or the politician that makes the decision and for whatever the reason they make it, the result has been pretty unfortunate. I think that this provides good opportunity for the sociologist to do very useful things, particularly in those parts of the world where people living in harmony is the exception rather than the rule.

D. Thorpe. Professor Johnson-Marshall mentioned the dichotomy between the politician and the planner. This should be very much a dialogue. Perhaps the planner does not often enough put the right case to the politician. This does mean getting into his shoes and not expecting him to be a planner. This surely is the normal procedure for anybody who is trying to influence the decision-maker.

W. F. Harris. I find it rather disturbing that the concept of planning is only associated with the hardware of society. I do not think you can plan a hardware of society *per se*, you must plan the hardware, along with the services, and with the whole pattern of life. Plans must be adaptable to the sheer pace and trend of human evolution. They are intertwined so you cannot cut them up into neat little compartments and have them all administered by different authorities, by classes of people like politicians and planners.

D. Lyddon. A great deal of the discussion has examined alternative models of the economic and the social pattern with the object of balancing the physical models. Planners are still being charged with producing physical attempts in the absence of the social and economic models, although the new attitude is of a greater involvement and intertwining of all possible skills.

One way of tackling the problem which we may be forced into, is that one should regard the physical model as a hypothesis; one should attempt to produce alternative hypotheses of the hardware, and then be in a position to measure this in the economic and social sense.

I think physical planners can do more in laying out the alternatives which would help the politicians by presenting them with feasible choices. What we are lacking is the ability to measure these alternatives against social and economic models.

Emrys Jones. One of the areas of greatest conflict I think lies in the notion of 'change'. It is quite obvious from Dr Ceccarelli's paper that this is absolutely fundamental. One is looking for some equilibrium and constantly there is change. On the other hand a planner is never happier than when producing a completely static model, an ideal city in fact. The difficulty is to allow for growth and change in a physical model. It is very easy to allow for this in the sociological model. Indeed most urban models that are being developed now are models of change and growth. To translate this into physical terms however is extremely difficult. Can you have such a situation? Each hospital must be planned, in which a brief cannot be given because change is so imminent and yet so unpredictable. You can never predict in which sector it will occur so you have to have a physical model which is capable of developing in any direction.

Here it seems to me is the greatest area of conflict, where the ideal of the planner is the static monolithic city once and for all and the ideal of the sociological planner, is constant change.

P. E. A. Johnson-Marshall. I do not really think planners have this philosophy. There is now a view of architectural planning which demands a kind of 'rubber city'. There has however to be a moment of commitment when the planner has to make a decision so that the architect can get on and actually commit society in terms of actual built environment. If this environment is to be built, inevitably it must remain static for a considerable period.

R. White. The rapid advance of mechanization in the countryside has led to a form of depopulation. A lot of this migration is daily, however; due to the rapid increase in transport, people can now commute from the agricultural areas where they probably used to earn a living, into the cities. This seems to be a special form of migration and urbanisation.

EC D

Ruth Glass. Professor White's point is reflected in our statistics. You have a much higher proportion of non-agricultural population, living in areas not classified as cities. Mechanization could bring about, especially in developing countries, even greater labour surplus than already exist in the countryside, thus causing further urbanization. Further internal migration of this kind would have consequences that might be serious, although I do not share some of the catastrophic predictions.

On Professor Emrys Jones' point about specific solutions, I think you have to be very careful because very often it is in fact no more than an insistence on leaving things as they are. This is why it is so very important to sort out the problems about which evaluation is not very difficult, and to do something about them.

On Mr Lyddon's point about the measurement of alternatives, we have a certain physical area and certain specified land uses to deal with. How do we measure the alternative implications for social structure or economic development. I do not think it is all that difficult provided that planners do not ask trivial questions. If you ask me, for instance, to tell how many red-haired men in Stevenage will beat their wives every second Saturday if you build and design houses in a certain way I cannot answer that – it is not possible. But there are many things that may be answered. One problem is to sort out the normal from the abnormal which I think is really the first job. We have had a lot of pseudo-sophistication and are continually worrying about the abnormal without really getting a bit clearer in our heads what the normal is.

Part Two . Economics

Urban Growth, Resources and Values
P. A. Stone, Natural Institute of Economic and Social Research, London

An Introduction to the Economics of Urban Growth
J. N. Wolfe, Professor of Economics, University of Edinburgh

Discussion :
Sir Robert Matthew, Professor of Architecture, University of Edinburgh
C. Blake, Professor of Economics, University of Dundee

The Approach of an Economist-Errant
J. Parry-Lewis, Professor of Town and Country Planning
University of Manchester

Urban Growth, Resources and Values

P. A. STONE

The population of Great Britain is expected to have increased by over a third by the early years of the next century. Even if only a moderate rate of increase in productivity is achieved, real wealth per head could be three times what it is today. Thus both the addition to the population and the basic population are likely to require urban facilities of a much higher standard than is generally available today. The population of working age, will, of course, increase but not as fast as the total population. If more young people are in full-time education, people retire earlier, work shorter hours and take longer holidays, the increase in working hours would be much less than the increase in the population of working age. Later retirement and a greater proportion of working wives would offset this to some extent. On the other hand, productivity is likely to rise in construction as well as elsewhere and there could be a shift of resources from other sectors of the economy to construction. Additional development and higher standards of development will also create a need to transfer a large amount of additional land from agricultural uses to urban uses.

To a large extent urban growth and development, and its location is determined by government action. In fact, at present about half of the expenditure on the built environment is directly to the account of the government and its agents and government action strongly influences the environment in which the private sector reaches its decisions. Government decisions are therefore of paramount importance in the determination of urban growth. They affect its scale, standards, forms, location and timing. The importance of reaching the best solutions in this field are further increased by the time it takes to create built environment, by the durability of development once created and by the time it takes to change the scale of construction if efficiency is not to be sacrificed.

The importance of this sector of the economy cannot be in doubt. In Great Britain it accounts for about a half of the fixed capital formation. About a twelfth of the gross national product is used in this way. Other western countries mostly use a greater proportion of their national product in this way, on average about a half more, although one or two countries use twice as much. However, even in Great Britain, the proportion rises to about an eighth when the maintenance and improvement work is added. The form and location of urban growth also, of course, influences the volume of national output.

It is clear that this is a field in which the market only provides limited indications of the preferences for the various types of built facility or of the full consequences of decisions about the use of resources. How under these conditions can the government determine the best policies to follow? In what way can it test the alternative policies which are open to it? Are the decisions which have been made satisfactory? Has the government the information and the decision techniques which are necessary to enable them to reach sound decisions in this field? These are some of the questions which I propose to raise in this paper.

SOME ECONOMIC CRITERIA

Three types of economic tests can be applied to urban developments, tests of the availability of resources, tests of the availability of finance and tests of value for money. The first type of test is concerned with the availability of land and with the capacity of the design, administrative manufacturing and construction sections of the economy to develop, redevelop and maintain the built environment required. The second type of test is concerned with the extent to which private and public finance will be available to facilitate the movement of resources. The extent to which finance will be available will depend on the way private persons and the community as a whole value the facilities and amenities to be provided and the extent to which this sense of values is reflected in the judgements of the government.

Clearly what is required is an assessment of both the costs and values associated with a range of policy options. The assessment of the direct cost of urban growth and of maintaining the stock of urban facilities is fairly straightforward. The assessment of all the side effects is more difficult, especially in a national or regional context. The assessment of values, in the sense of satisfactions, presents considerable problems.

A more practical, although less ambitious, starting-point is to evaluate the costs of policy options defined in terms of scales, standards, forms and locations. For example, the costs could be assessed of providing given types of facility, at given standards and forms for the population of Great Britain, a region or a town. Separate estimates could be prepared for different levels of standard and different forms. While no direct measure of value is obtained, some concept of value can be associated with each policy option, through its definition in terms of scale, standard and form. It is possible to estimate which pattern of options is feasible in terms of the resources and finance available, and to consider which patterns of options provide the best value for money.

In the sector for the built environment building standards could perhaps be defined in terms of space, quality and equipment, road standards to terms of speed, safety and capacity, and public utility standards in terms of capacity and amenity. Clearly this form of assessment could be extended over other parts of the economy. For example, educational standards could perhaps be defined in terms of the opportunity to attend each level of education and the probability of reaching an adequate standard within it, and defence standards in terms of the probabilities of success in preventing and triumphing in various sorts of conflicts. Appropriate definitions could be worked out according to the nature of the sector and the narrowness with which it was to be defined.

Such a system appears to offer a comparatively simple way of comparing various combinations of goals in which there is some way of visualizing the values created as well as of comparing the resources required and the feasibility of providing them.

THE REQUIREMENTS FOR HOUSING IN GREAT BRITAIN

Housing is one of the easiest sectors in which to apply this type of analysis and it is convenient to consider possible policies for housing as an illustration of the technique suggested. The Registrars General have projected that over the period 1964 – 2004 the population of Great Britain will increase from about 53 million to about 72 million. The increase in population depends, of course, very much on the rate of birth, which is very volatile. The population could increase to as much as 85 million or to as little as 65 million. These figures can be taken as bench marks. The rates of household formation are also likely to rise. With a population of 72 million there might be about 24 million households. The number of households is, of course, far less affected in the short run by changes in birth rates than is population. The corresponding bench marks for households would be just over 26 million and just over 23 million. Since some part of the stock would always be vacant and some households would require second homes, the number of dwellings required might be perhaps a million more than the number of households.

In 1964, there were about 16·8 million dwellings in existence, so that the number of additional dwellings likely to be required over the period 1965 – 2004 would be perhaps about 8 million. Of course, many of the dwellings in the present stock are very old, and many are likely to become obsolete over the period because of the difficulty and cost of adapting them to current standards. Many also are in a poor condition and lack the facilities now considered essential, although short-term improvement would be possible and economic in the majority of cases. In the absence of information about the types of dwellings in the stock, age is perhaps the best indicator of the likely scale of obsolescence. If the equivalent of all but the best pre-1881 dwellings were to be replaced, about 4·6 million dwellings would be needed. If the bench mark was taken as pre-1921 dwellings, the figure would be about 7·4 million, while if pre-1941 dwellings were taken the figure would be 11·5 million. Thus the number of dwellings to be built over the period 1964 to 2004 depends far more on the rate of replacement than on the rate at which the population increases.

Since 1964, about a million and a half dwellings have been built and about 400,000 have been demolished, so that now the stock stands at about 18 million. By the end of the current decade it is expected that there will be a broad balance between the number of households and the number of dwellings, although there may be some local shortages. Over the next decade 150,000 dwellings a year are expected to provide an adequate addition to the stock. In fact, unless birth rates or households increase faster than is expected 180,000 dwellings a year over the period to 2004 would provide about a million more dwellings than households.

The number of dwellings required for replacing the existing stock is more problematic. On average about 120,000 dwellings a year would be sufficient to replace all but the best pre-1881 dwellings, while 190,000 a year would be sufficient to replace all but the best pre-1921 dwellings. At present about 30,000 dwellings a year are used to replace dwellings lost in the course of road and town developments. In the long run most of these would be included in the number replaced because of age.

Thus at the current rate of construction there would be sufficient dwellings by 2004 to replace the majority of those built before 1921. If construction continues at this rate during the next decade, replacement could proceed at three times the current rate. To achieve this rate considerable changes in the administration of housing would be necessary.

In order to trace the consequences of the current housing policy further, it is, of course, necessary to estimate the resources that would be required. Perhaps the most interesting point which emerges is the relationship between the resources required for new construction and for maintenance work.

If the standards of basic housing are set at the Parker-Morris levels and the current scales of standards and current forms are assumed, the estimated cost at 1964 prices of 11·6 million dwellings, enough to replace most pre-1881 dwellings by 2004, would be about £40 thousand million.

Even though the older dwellings would be replaced over the period it would still be economically worthwhile to repair and improve many of them in order to provide housing in the meantime sufficiently comparable in standard to Parker Morris housing. This would probably cost between £5 and £6 thousand millions. The addition of garages would add over £3 thousand million to this figure. The poor condition of large numbers of dwellings in the stock and their lack of facilities is well established. The cost of repairing and improving them is not surprising. More surprising perhaps is the inadequacy of the current standards of housing maintenance which are reflected by the condition of the stock.

The amount spent on maintenance in real terms in recent years has been falling while the size of the stock has been rising. Currently maintenance expenditure is on average not more than a third of what the cost would be on the basis considered necessary for public authority dwellings. This standard makes little provision for decoration and for the type of improvements usually carried out by the householder's own labour. On this scale the costs of regular maintenance over the period would be about £38 thousand million, nearly as much as the cost of new work.

If maintenance were to be carried out on this scale and the condition of the existing stock were to be raised to current standards over the next decade, in so far as this was economic, it would be necessary to spend as much on maintenance work as is now spent on all housing work. The feasibility of improving housing on this scale depends on resources likely to be required for other construction work, on the probable output of construction work and on the resources which might be moved into this sector from elsewhere.

THE REQUIREMENTS FOR OTHER BUILT ENVIRONMENT

Similar models can, of course, be built as a basis of estimating the resources required for each aspect of the built environment. Broadly they follow a similar pattern of projecting population, activity rates, space and other standards and combining them to provide estimates of space needs. These can be compared with estimates of the stock of built facilities to provide a measure of the facilities which need to be constructed. These can subsequently be costed to provide a measure of resources likely to be required. Allowance must, of course, be made for such interactions as those between road and town redevelopment and for the condition and potential of the stock, and the necessary work of replacement, maintenance and improvement.

While such models have been prepared results are available at present only for housing. Preliminary work indicates that housing represents between a third and a half of the total costs of the development, redevelopment and maintenance of the built environment. Again, because of the inadequate standards of much of the built environment, a large proportion of the work on non-residential facilities is likely to be urgent and problems of priority cannot be avoided.

Preliminary estimates indicate that the total resources required for all urban growth, redevelopment and maintenance over the period 1965 – 2004 at 1964 prices might be between £190 and £240 thousand million. The amount will depend, of course, on the standard and forms selected, on the size of the population and on where development takes place.

The estimates are based on the assumption that the standards considered appropriate today would continue to be acceptable and that the rates of redevelopment would be rather faster than in the past. Changes in these assumptions would, of course, result in considerable changes in the estimates. For example, the estimate for new dwellings given above as about 140 thousand million would be increased by about £10 thousand million if pre-1921 instead of pre-1881 dwellings were to be replaced. A further £17 thousand million would be added if pre-1941 dwellings were to be replaced during the period discussed. On the other hand, all these figures would be reduced by about an eighth if the standards of dwellings were reduced to those accepted prior to the introduction of the Parker-Morris standards. Again, if one third, rather than two thirds, of existing non-residential buildings were replaced during the period costs might be reduced by about £12 thousand million. There would, of course, be a consequential reduction in expenditure on road improvement and in the scale and standards of roads which could be made available, since less cleared land would be available for redevelopment.

In the long run standards for the built environment appear likely to rise broadly in step with rises in the standard of living. If the standards of all parts of the built environment were to be kept in step with probable increases in the standard of living, this would add considerably to the resources required. For example, standards would be more than doubled over 40 years if they increased at 2 per cent a year. If this happened, in the case of housing, the standard of the better class as distinct from the luxury class dwelling of today would become the basic dwelling. This does not appear to be unlikely.

The form of development also affects the resources required.

High rise housing is about fifty per cent more expensive than low rise housing. Generally multi-level development adds to the resources required whether for buildings or developments. Decked shopping and service cores appear to be about five times as expensive as cores developed on the ground. Multi-storey car parks are ten times as expensive as hardstanding on the ground. Elevated urban motorways appear to be about seven times as expensive as roads on the ground and bored tunnels about fifty times as expensive. The shape, layout and size of settlements also affects the amount of resources required.

Resource requirements are also affected by location, partly because of site conditions, partly because of the effect of redeveloping existing urban facilities and partly because prices are higher in some areas than others.

The form of development and the rate of rebuilding the existing stock will also affect the amount of additional land required for urban growth. This might average at around 1·6 million acres. The amount would, of course, depend on the forms of development. For example, the area of land required for housing at current densities might be about 0·6 million acres but it might be two thirds greater or a third less depending on the density of development. Up to a point more land would also be required if the rate of replacing the stock was increased.

THE RESOURCES AVAILABLE

Over the last 7 or 8 years the construction sector of the building industry appears to have increased its average annual productivity in new work by about 3·0 to 3·5 per cent. In maintenance work the figure is probably only about 1·0 to 1·5 per cent. The measurement of output in design work is much more difficult but it is doubtful whether productivity has increased as much as in new work. The manufacture of materials and components is, of course, spread over many industries. In general they have probably achieved increases in productivity comparable with those achieved in new construction. The supply of innovations in management, construction techniques and component development, which has given rise to these increases in productivity, is nothing like spent. The rate at which firms adopt innovations is inevitably slow in an established industry. It appears likely, that even if there are not revolutionary changes in this sector, productivity will continue to increase for many years. Output per man-year will of course be affected by changes in the hours of work and in holidays. Unless there are revolutionary changes in design, construction techniques, or organization, it would appear to be optimistic to expect productivity per man-year to rise more than perhaps 4 per cent for new work and 2 per cent for maintenance work.

Over 40 years, such increases would result in the output per man-year rising by a factor of nearly 5 in the case of new work and over 2 in maintenance work. The value of annual output is already twice as great in new work as in maintenance work. If these rates of productivity were obtained the difference in the value of output of new and maintenance work would be nearly fivefold by the end of the period. Such changes would have a radical effect on the proportion of operatives used in each type of work. For example, whereas now there are more than a third more operatives on new housing work than on housing maintenance, by the end of the period, the number of operatives on housing maintenance would be several times greater than those on new work. The greater the amount of housing maintenance work to be done relative to new work, the direction suggested earlier, the greater this shift in proportions would be. The result of transferring labour from a sector of relatively high productivity to a sector of relatively low productivity, would be to depress the average increase in output per man-year. As a result the rate of rise of productivity might even be below that expected for maintenance work. Of course, if this occurred the number of dwellings worth improving as compared with replacing would fall and thus shift the ratios of labour more in favour of new work.

It would appear that much more attention should be given to the organization of maintenance work and to the development of building techniques and building components which would facilitate maintenance and improvement.

At most the average rate of growth of working population over the period is not expected to be more than about three quarters per cent per year and this rate may be reduced by changes in working habits and in education. The construction sector might not, of course, even be able to maintain its present proportion of the labour force.

Armed with information of this type it is possible to examine development policy, to determine which policies are feasible and which appear to require an excessive sacrifice of other desirable ends.

THE IMPLICATIONS FOR HOUSING POLICIES

The rates of increase in productivity and in the labour force given above might not be sufficient to enable the housing sector to carry out the programmes of construction and improvement on the scale indicated earlier. The balance between the supply and demand for housing appears to be sensitive to the rate of replacing the stock of dwellings and the consequential changes in maintenance and improvement work, and to the priority given to replacement and maintenance work. The greater the priority given to the latter, the greater the total value of work likely to be completed. It would appear that unless the proportion of resources devoted to housing is increased, it would not be possible to replace more than pre-1881 dwellings by the end of the period considered. This would imply about 300,000 dwellings a year on average over the period. Even so it would not be possible to provide full maintenance standards for all the dwellings in the stock.

While the construction of dwellings at the current rate over the next decade would enable the rate of replacement of unsatisfactory dwellings to be increased threefold, it would still take over a decade to replace the dwellings 'currently' in the worst class, those with structural failures and serious physical deterioration. If in the meantime arrears of maintenance are not made good and regular maintenance is not carried out at an adequate standard, more dwellings will deteriorate beyond the point at which repair is worthwhile and it may be two or three decades before even dwellings in the poorest condition are eliminated and all households can be housed adequately.

It might be thought reasonable to aim over the next decade at clearing urgent housing improvement work and raising the standards of the regular maintenance of housing to the level suggested as acceptable. To achieve this an immediate increase of output in construction as a whole would be required of about an eighth, as well as a continuation of increase in output as great as in the recent past.

It appears unlikely that, in a period in which there is pressure to increase exports and replace capital equipment as well as for more consumption of other goods and services, additional resources would be moved into construction on the scale required. The pressures for new urban growth, and replacement and improvement in the non-residential sector of the urban environment are probably no less than for housing and it appears unlikely that resources on an adequate scale could be transferred to the housing sector.

Thus if more resources are to be devoted to the maintenance and improvement of housing, fewer resources will be available for new construction. For example, half the additional resources required could be obtained by reducing constructions to about 300,000 dwellings a year. Further resources could be obtained by concentrating on the most economic forms of development. While the resources which could be made available in this way would not enable the standards of regular ma intenance to be raised to the required level over the next decade, it w ould be possible to make good the condition of the existing stoc k and to provide adequate facilities for dwellings likely to remain in use for some time.

A short-t erm policy of reducing the rate of new constructions would not, in the circumstances visualised, prejudice the number of dwellings constructed in the long run, since the longer their construction is delayed, the less resources would be required to construct each dwelling.

It is clear that if these assumptions prove to be correct, there would be no possibility of raising the standards of housing above those taken as representing the current best standards, or of adopting more expensive forms of development on any scale, unless additional resources could be obtained from other sectors of the economy.

REGIONAL PROBLEMS

Similar types of analysis are necessary at both the regional and local level.

Some regions are worse off than others both because the stock is comparatively older and in a poorer condition, and because the labour force currently available is smaller relative to needs as compared with other regions. For example, on the basis of the assumptions given for the housing sector, it would appear that the South-East and East Anglia might need to release construction capacity to other regions, particularly to Scotland and the North-West.

Clearly regional development plans need to be tested against the resources required. Valid comparisons between alternatives can hardly be made until the feasibility of providing the resources is established. Some preliminary studies suggest that it may not be feasible to provide resources for both the urban growth, and the renewal and improvement of the existing urban fabric within the timetables suggested.

Land is probably more of a regional problem than a national one. The land estimated to be required for urban development over the 40 year period amounts to about 5 per cent of the present area of arable and grassland in Great Britain. Since farm output per acre is increasing rapidly, the loss of output from land taken over the forty-year period is likely to be made good in two or three years. The effect of increases in population on the demand for home grown food far exceeds the effect of land lost to development. However, the best agricultural land not only already yields about three times as much per acre as average land but yields appear to be rising faster on the better land. It is, therefore, unwise to use such land and certainly unwise to use a disproportionate amount of it. On the other hand, land less suitable for farming is frequently difficult to develop and it may not be economic to incur the additional costs. Some regions are endowed with better land than others, and it may be difficult in some areas to find sufficient low grade land suitable for development. Similarly there is a very uneven distribution of land suitable for recreational purposes.

For these reasons, difficulties are likely to be met if too much further development takes place in the more highly populated regions.

Of course, against such considerations it is necessary to set some measure of the comparative industrial advantages and personal satisfactions from urban development in different locations.

THE IMPLEMENTATION OF POLICIES

It is not, of course, sufficient for governments, whether central, regional or local to select policy options for urban growth and development simply on grounds of the standards they would provide and the availability of resources, although these would appear to be necessary criteria. There could be no assurance that such policies would be implemented, even if the government had correctly reflected the communities consensus of opinion on the returns they would provide. The decisions taken about the use of resources by those responsible for their use might lead to the movement of resources in a pattern quite inappropriate to the implementation of the policies which had been selected. The government has still to create an economic environment in harmony with the requirements for the implementation of the chosen policies.

Generally the range of standards selected by those responsible for decisions for the built environment will be far wider than those which would be selected centrally on welfare grounds. There is a tendency by those responsible for decisions on development to attach more importance to the standards of new facilities than to the standards of existing ones and to ignore economies external to them.

In the business sector an urban facility is a factor of production. Its value lies in the contribution it makes to the productive process and to the surplus on the capital employed. The value to the user will tend only to be of consequence if this affects production costs or revenue. This will set a limit to the standard which the occupier will find worth purchasing. The standard will vary with the type of business and with its level of efficiency. The amount worth spending will usually be judged after allowance for taxation. Because of the incidence of taxation and because it is often difficult to obtain capital, standards of construction often tend to be depressed. Frequently expenditure on buildings appears to be judged against turnover rather than against the resulting returns, so that buildings housing efficient firms in types of businesses with large turnovers per unit area tend to be opulent while at the other extreme those housing marginal firms in types of businesses producing little value per unit area tend to be squalid.

In the personal sector the value of a building arises not from a money revenue but from the satisfactions enjoyed by the occupier. The price he is prepared to pay in order to increase these satisfactions inevitably depends on income as well as on the relative scale of values. Again the range of standards thought acceptable will be very wide. The propensity to spend on urban facilities can be raised by grants and tax relief which increases the resources available, and by shifting taxes to other goods and services which tends to raise the comparative value of the satisfactions obtained from expenditure on urban facilities.

Buildings and development in the public sector are provided partly for the use of industrial and commercial organizations, partly for organizations providing a social or administrative service and partly directly for use by the public. Nationalized industries and public authority trading services are generally expected to provide something near a commercial return on the capital they employ. Hence their criteria for building standards will not be dissimilar to those of business organizations. Other public organizations tend to be in a different position from either business or personal occupiers of urban facilities. They are not responsible for raising the resources needed, and frequently do not occupy the facilities provided. The resources for built facilities tend to be allocated separately from those for other purposes and frequently the resources allocated for construction are separate from those for the maintenance and operation of the facilities. Consequently it is in the interest of the occupiers to press for the highest possible standards. The administrators determining the standards are frequently separate from those responsible for providing resources, which are determined globally and have little experience in the use of the facilities, and hence have no adequate grounds on which to assess satisfactions. It is not surprising in these circumstances that all too frequently the standards set for new facilities are too high in relation to the resources available for their national provision and too high in relation to the standards possible with the resources available for maintaining existing facilities. Thus again the range of standards is very wide and new facilities tend to be at much higher standards than those of the stock of facilities on which most people depend.

THE PROBLEM OF MEASURING VALUES

It is clear that the goal of maximising the return on resources is impeded by the difficulty of measuring values. In the business sector and in the personal sector the problems are not too difficult. In the business sector costs and values can both be expressed in money terms. In the personal sector costs can similarly be evaluated in money terms. While the occupier cannot necessarily express his evaluation of the satisfactions quantitatively, he can at least decide whether their comparative price is high or low. There are, of course, frequently statistical difficulties in the measurement of costs and values. Again in that part of the public sector concerned with production and distribution the analytical problems are not so different from those in the business sector. Elsewhere in the public sector the measurement of costs is more difficult because it is necessary to consider the way the side effects change the use of resources. However, the greatest difficulties lie in the evaluation of the satisfactions derived from facilities for which, in this sector, there are no market prices. This difficulty appears likely to grow as real wealth grows and urban policy options are less concerned with the scales of provision and more with standards, forms and locations, and as choice lies increasingly between options some of which provide a basis for new and un-experienced life styles.

Since in the final resort government action is concerned not only with the public sector but also with the private sector, decisions at this level tend to embrace the whole economy. The problem is to measure the satisfactions likely to be obtained from marginal changes in expenditure on, for example, consumer goods and services, leisure, social services, security services and justice, and the built environment. In the latter field the problem is to compare satisfactions obtained by raising the standards of one or two types of facility as compared with others, for example, housing and hospitals, as compared with schools, work places, recreation places and roads. Again there is the problem of comparing the satisfactions from the life styles possible in different urban forms, for example, in houses with gardens as compared with flats, in large as compared with small towns and in towns catering for personal as compared with public transport. Similar problems arise in comparing one location with another.

The area for which there is a lack of indications of the consumers' valuation could, of course, be reduced by extending the range of urban facilities handled through the market. For example, the market for low cost housing could be recreated. Many urban facilities are essentially collective goods but techniques can often be devised for creating a market. Tolls can easily be collected for the use of motorways and bridges, and could be extended to the use of country parks and other large recreational facilities. Methods of charging drivers for the use of road space in cities have also been suggested. Often, however, the provision of urban facilities result in more benefits to the public at large than to the direct users and charging the latter would provide little measure of the total satisfactions derived. Frequently too the costs of collecting charges are unreasonable in relation to the advantages obtained. While the use of the market

EC E

provides both a measure of value and a direct link between demand and supply, unless there is a considerable degree of equality of income, a large part of the community may in practice be excluded from the facilities provided by the market. This difficulty can be overcome in a number of ways, for example, for providing grants to members of the community with inadequate incomes and by providing all members of the community with a ration of points which can be used as the means of gaining admittance to a certain range of facilities – for instance, rural recreational facilities. The market does not, however, provide any measure of satisfactions likely to be derived from new forms of facility. More experimentation with urban forms would enable users to obtain a wider experience and to express their valuations.

Even if market techniques are exploited more widely, there will remain a large field of facilities for which techniques for measuring values will be required. Many techniques have been suggested and are in use, for example, the questioning of users, the observation of the way users adapt to given conditions and studying the way users arrange alternatives in terms of value. Other methods depend more on professional evaluation, for example, by a system of pointing. While the experts are likely to have a better appreciation of the implications of alternative forms and standards than the users, their scales of values may not be the same.

Too few of the standards commonly used in urban planning appear to have any firm basis. Until more is known about the satisfactions obtained from different standards and forms of urban facility, it is difficult to determine which policy options would provide the best returns.

CONCLUSIONS

The scales, standards, forms and location of urban growth and the urban stock are determined to a considerable extent in a sophisticated society by decisions taken within the government machine. If satisfactory returns are to be obtained from the resources used, a thorough understanding of the implication of the urban options is necessary. The comparison of the implications of alternative options measured in terms of scales, standards, forms and location and their testing against the availability of resources appears to provide a useful starting point and at least provides an indication of feasibility and of the action which needs to be taken to implement decisions. It does not, however, provide an adequate means of comparing returns. Until satisfactions can be measured with reasonable accuracy, the quality of decisions about urban facilities are likely to be inadequate. The development of techniques for evaluating urban standards and urban choice would appear to be a field in which the social sciences should take an increasing interest.

The estimates given in this paper have been obtained in the course of research carried out at the National Institute of Economic and Social Research. The work has been financed by the Nuffield Foundation. The Institute will publish the full results in P.A. Stone, *Urban Development in Britain: Standards, Costs and Resources, 1964 – 2004* (Cambridge University Press).

An Introduction to the Economics of Urban Growth

J. N. WOLFE

The first points to mention about the economics of urban growth are the facts of the situation. Not many months ago, the opinion was firmly held that the population of the United Kingdom would grow by approximately 40 per cent, to about 75 million, by the end of the century. Within a twelve-month period, that prospect has shrunk and now one gathers the new official view is that it will only grow by 16 million. This has thrown many calculations into some degree of confusion.

With this basic problem of population growth, there is also the fact of urbanization. Some say that urbanization is no longer apparent in Western Europe and that cities are no longer growing. It, in fact, turns out that this is a question of definition and that in some sense cities continue to grow. Certainly, if we look at the longer term position in this country, say going back 150 years, it will be found that most of the major cities in this country were quite small towns. Urbanization is distinctly a phenomenon which was most striking in the nineteenth century, but which goes on today in a slightly different form in the growth of suburban areas and areas somewhat outwith the town.

The third fact that we have to bear in mind as a background to the discussion of the economics of urban growth is the regional shift of population. It turns out that while the 'drift to the south-east' may in some sense be an illusion, certain regions of the country and in particular Scotland and the north are growing more slowly, if at all, whereas the regions further south do appear to be growing in population rather more rapidly. There is some question of whether this population growth in itself is not really the effect of immigration from overseas and I leave it to the sociologists to enquire whether a continuation of growth from that source is either likely or desirable. The fact is that so far, at any rate, large chunks of the country have not had the population growth which we have seen in the so-called 'coffin' from London to Manchester. Colin Clark has made the extremely interesting point that, while everybody says the world is becoming overpopulated and that this is a great economic disaster, there is nothing that pains a region more than to find its population is not growing as quickly as everybody else's population. It is a striking fact that all the political forces in this country are organized on the basis of obtaining a fair share of population increase, and, in particular, this is true for Scotland.

We then have to ask ourselves which are the basic issues which confront us in the economics of urban growth; I think there are three basic issues. The first one is whether we shall confine our cities within some kind of limits either in terms of population or in terms of a physical limitation imposed by a green belt. Secondly, there is the question of whether population growth shall be organized in large or small communities. While this is partly a sociological and political issue – it is from many points of view predominantly an economic issue. Finally, there is the question of the extent to which we are to leave the natural forces of the economy to increase the dominance of the London-Manchester axis, or the extent to which we will develop our policy for urban growth, with a diminution of the weight of the London-Manchester axis as a prime consideration. Our attitude to the London-Manchester axis has a pronounced influence upon the decisions which we ought to make with respect to the other policy issues.

Now let me touch upon the means which are available for the implementation of urban growth policy. Obviously a very large part of urban policy is determined in the two principal government departments charged with these matters – the Ministry of Housing and Local Government on the one hand, and the Scottish Development Department on the other. But there are, in practice, certain other organizations, to some degree subsidiary but partly independent, which play an important role and may in the future play a much more important role in urban growth. The obvious things to mention here are, of course, the New Town Corporations and the Scottish Special Housing Association. The latter, I think, has no English equivalent, but it is an extremely useful device for facilitating urban growth in a form and in places which are socially attractive but are not particularly attractive to the Local Authorities involved. There are also fiscal instruments for regional economic policy, in particular the Regional Employment Premium, which is now very significant, and differential grants for capital construction. On top of these we must mention too the grants and loans under the Local Employment Act. These mechanisms for direction of industry are intended primarily for directing industry towards the Development Areas. The Development Areas, however, are rather large, and these fiscal instruments do not provide a very sensitive tool for influencing development within them, nor have they provided a useful tool for dealing with the problems of places outside the development areas but also outside the London-Manchester axis. The Hunt Committee has been set up to consider what can be done about the difficulties which are increasingly being experienced by these areas, which are known as the 'grey areas' as distinct from the Development Areas, which are presumably 'black'.

We must mention next the Long Term Population Distribution Committee whose endeavours – at an inter-departmental level – have resulted in rather spectacular bursts of activity. It has been responsible in particular for the formulation of the three super-proposals for urban growth in the United Kingdom – the proposals for cities of one million population on Severnside and Humberside and for the expansion of Dundee to a city approaching half a million. These proposals are a special case of a general phenomenon : the utilization of infrastructure investment (which is largely outside the control of Local Authorities) as a means of stimulating development in particular localities.

I have not mentioned the Industrial Development Certificates, although these are widely believed to be the most important of all the instruments available for influencing the location of economic activity. They will be discussed in some detail later in the paper.

Let us consider the alternatives which confront us if we decide that cities will be constrained by physical limitation – that is, a policy of rigid green belts. Around London where a fairly rigid green belt has been enforced there has been the development of what is called an 'urban halo', that is to say, the development of a large band of built up area lying just beyond the green belt. The development of the 'urban halo' and the transportation networks needed to provide access to the 'urban halo' raise in a very clear form the question of the purpose of the green belt. If the green belt is to be surrounded by a built-up area, is there really much point in having it? Its value as agricultural land is diminished, it has never really been conceived as a recreational area in the full sense, and it would be very big to be maintained as a park. Consequently many people say that the green belt, as far as rapidly expanding places are concerned, is an anomalous and unnecessary restriction. There is a further point. If one is to restrict the physical size of a city, it becomes imperative that, with a growth in its population, one provides a substantial proportion of housing in denser form. This means providing housing in the form of high rise buildings. These are extremely expensive. Dr Stone has mentioned a premium of 50 per cent per square foot for high rise buildings.

It is admittedly not only the green belt which has caused the construction of high rise buildings. It is partly the result of what we may call jurisdictional difficulties among Local Authorities. Probably the limitations on the size of the administrative units may have more to do with rather wasteful building of this form than has the green belt, and this problem may be diminished if there is a reorganization of local government on regional lines.

If we impose green belt restrictions on our cities, and if the cities continue to attract population, and if we eschew high density housing, then we bring upon ourselves a problem of overspill of population. This raises the possibility of constructing satellite towns, which are usually satellite new towns around the restricted city. This involves substantial costs, which can be calculated, costs in terms of extra travel facilities, of time spent in travelling to work, in terms of high rise buildings, and so on. The advantages are rather less clear but it would be possible to conduct cost benefit analyses of them. My initial surmise would be that the green belt restricted city is remarkably cost ineffective. This is perhaps one of the reasons why thinking has moved rapidly away from the satellite new town. The green belt, as we have known it in the past, reflects an ideology of diminishing importance.

If we are going to allow our cities to expand, we have to consider what alternative forms this may take. Here the economic issues become rather more clear cut. It is possible to consider and evaluate in an economic way each of the main alternatives. We may allow our cities to expand in what I call a circular pattern, that is to say that we add housing and buildings generally to our cities without leaving any large amount of open space between the built up areas. This is a characteristic of cities built up during the nineteenth century. The second possibility is that we remove all controls and allow what is known as 'urban sprawl' to develop. 'Urban sprawl' is the result of the free development of cities under the impact of the motor car. This procedure brings economic forces into full play and provides the minimum amount of restriction and the minimum amount of red tape. It is, however, unacceptable on aesthetic grounds. The third possibility, which has been identified to a considerable degree with the plan for the expansion of the city of Paris, is what is known as the 'starfish' or 'starshape' city. It is the extension of our present more or less round cities by rather long arms which allow the intervening spaces to be held as green areas or parkland. This 'starfish' city does allow the possibility of continuous growth and it has been attractive to many administrators and some planners. The next possibility is the city which I think is best described as the 'doughnut' city. The development at Peterborough appears on the face of it to be an approach to this conception. The 'doughnut' city consists of taking an urban area and adding extensions to it in the form of long arms going both north and south but enclosing finally a large park area which is contiguous to the existing central city. It will be seen that that style of development is a very attractive one from the point of view of access to park area as well as the form of road system. Finally, we come to the kind of development which is probably most popular in Britain at the moment, but about which I am somewhat less enthusiastic from the economic point of view, and that is the so-called nodal development, the development of cities by the creation of smaller communities outside the original built-up area but connected to it by means of transport facilities, particularly roads.

Each of these systems can be costed. The two most important costs that arise are the costs of congestion on the one hand, particularly striking where the extension lies fairly close to the existing built-up area, and the costs of road systems and transport systems where developments lie somewhat further afield. There is further the question of the cost of travel to work, to shopping and to recreation, and these are seldom at the moment evaluated. There is a tendency to rank city development at the moment in terms only of visible costs rather than in terms of costs and benefits, and I am fairly sure that a careful examination, which considers both costs and benefits, is likely to overturn the order of preference which we would otherwise give to different city expansion forms.

Quite apart from these questions, there is the question of the attractiveness of different city forms to industry. The cities in the United Kingdom have suffered hitherto from the nineteenth-century system of location of industry rather close to the centre of the city. This location of industry does allow a maximum interpenetration of the city by the workforce living in the periphery, using public transport. It involves, however, substantial congestion which was, in the past, perhaps rather less important when railway transport represented the principal means of bringing in supplies and moving out finished goods. This situation has changed and it would seem that a good deal more enquiry needs to be done upon the costs, real or imaginary, to industry and particularly manufacturing industry of the form which city expansion takes. These costs are almost never calculated explicitly by the planner who is deciding on city form. They do appear implicitly in the form of pressure from the manufacturing and economic interests but it is not at all clear that these pressures are correctly evaluated; it is commonly the case that maximum pressure is exerted by firms already in the area whereas what one should be most concerned with is the economic advantage to the new man who may move to the town. This is an important issue which ought to have a strong influence on the way in which we develop our cities but which under present physical planning arrangements is almost totally neglected.

Indeed, we may go further and say that in a mixed economy without direction of industry, the creation of a climate attractive to incoming industry represents an objective equal in validity and importance to cost considerations, or indeed to considerations of amenity. There will, of course, in effect be a trade-off among these goals. The essential point in this paper, however, is that this trade-off is likely in practice to leave the attraction of industry as one of the most important elements in the priorities of any settlement away from the London-Manchester axis.

It is a widely accepted aim of policy to divert population growth away from the Manchester-London axis and development area policy is partly related to this issue. It is clear that this diversion of population can only be accomplished if we are able to divert industry away from the Manchester-London axis. It turns out that it is very difficult to divert industry in spite of the whole galaxy of regional employment policies, regional employment premium, investment grants and so on. It turns out that these mechanisms for moving industry are relatively ineffective. It turns out that the basic instrument hitherto has been the stick of the Industrial Development Certificate, the IDC, and it is widely believed that the elimination of IDC's would mean the almost complete breakdown of regional economic policy and of movement away from London and the Midlands.

The most striking aspect of economic location is the fact that industry prefers to move to localities having a large labour market and a large degree of ancillary and subsidiary service industry. It is extremely difficult to get industry to move to small labour markets, as Professor Johnson-Marshall and I know very well from our studies in the Central Borders. Since it is so difficult and since the system of regional employment premium does have such a limited effect and since we are determined to see that industry does not all settle in the London-Manchester axis – since all these things are true, then it would appear to be essential that housing and population policy outside the Manchester-London axis should concentrate upon the creation of large concentrated labour markets and therefore upon large centres of population. This point helps explain why the government is considering the creation of much larger new settlements than hitherto. If one wishes to persuade industry to move away from the London – Manchester axis one has to give industry the opportunity of moving to a large city. There is no point in creating new small communities to add to the list of potential disaster areas.

I return now to the question of the desirability of the system of IDC control. The Hunt Committee on the 'grey' areas has been be-sieged by representations from manufacturers and from regions in the south and Midlands objecting strenuously to the continuation of IDC control. In fact IDC control does not represent a very effective sieve : a rather large part of industrial investment continues to take place in the heavily industrialized London-Manchester area. What then is the basis of the objections to IDC's? Partly, it is simply the natural reluctance of people to be pushed about. Partly, it arises be-cause there is no established set of principles upon which IDC's are granted or withheld. This is effectively a question for negotiation be-tween the relevant officer of the Board of Trade and the industrialist involved, and as a result there is quite frequently the feeling among industrialists that they have somehow or other been discriminated against in the granting of an IDC. This is a characteristic of any direct control of this sort, particularly one where there is no accumulation of case law and where things are decided very much in terms of bar-gaining. The abandonment of IDC's is, of course, opposed by the development areas. The development areas feel that if any extra in-dustry is to be provided either for them or for the 'grey' areas, the system of IDC controls must be tightened rather than loosened. In my view, the situation is a dangerous one. The forces opposed to the IDC's are very strong, and unless something is done to appease them the system may become politically unworkable and have to be abandoned. There is however an alternative system, and not a very complicated one. This would consist of the auctioning of IDC certificates to the highest bidder. The proceeds of the auction could either go directly to the general revenue of the government or might be earmarked for the support of development areas. This is not a system which is particularly attractive to the administrator because he feels that it would discriminate in favour of the large and pros-perous firm. His view is that the large and prosperous firm is the kind which the development area needs most, and if IDC control were to be put on an auction basis few large firms might be forced to move. On the other hand, the alternative to it might prove in practice to be the abandonment of the system of IDC control as a whole. It would be difficult to envisage a sufficiently high rate of regional employ-ment premium or investment grant to achieve an equivalent effect.

To return to the question of large and small towns : it is said that a town on a green field site of a fairly modest size in the order of 100,000 population provides the lowest cost size for a new town. These cost figures are largely beside the point because the balance is properly one of costs and benefits. There is a feeling in Whitehall, and in the country as a whole, that the small community of 100,000 does not provide the range of services or the attractions as a community that larger communities can provide. There is the further point that it is not likely to attract industry at all easily. There is a counter indication in the success of the satellite new towns of the forties and fifties. Few of these towns have grown to as much as 100,000 and yet they have been eminently successful in attracting industry and they have been apparently successful in attracting population of high quality. Without being dogmatic, however, I would suggest that the success of the satellite new towns has arisen not so much because they were new or because they were the size they were but because they were satellites, because the population in them in fact was dependent to a very large degree both for jobs and for service facilities on the large cities near them. We know, for example, that the work composition of the city of Cumbernauld is such that a a very large proportion of the population of Cumbernauld does not work in Cumbernauld but works in the city of Glasgow. There is a similar labour movement between Glasgow and the factories of Cumbernauld. The question is still open whether a smallish new community which is not satellite could attract industry. There are one or two examples of success. The most striking one is probably at Glenrothes in Fife. There are however very special circumstances in this case associated with the attitude of Fife County Council which are not easily replicated elsewhere.

The question of the cash outlay involved in building towns of smaller size is not then the only consideration. In any event costs vary widely with road pattern and location. Investigation on this matter in the Central Borders study suggests that the differentials among alternative sites within the Central Borders, for example, are quite small relative to the differentials between building in the Central Borders and building, say, in the south-west. Many of the apparent differentials between costs in rebuilding or expanding old cities, compared with the cost of construction on green field sites, are a function of the particular road system and the particular configuration that one adopts and I offer the conjecture that this will be more important in practice than will the size of the new city.

My last topic is in some ways the most controversial. I want to talk for just a little while about development policy in Scotland. I do this mainly because development policy in Scotland is recognized to be the most advanced in the United Kingdom. We have in many ways pioneered in Scotland in regional development policy, population movement policy, and in industrial location policy. This has partly been possible because we have had for quite a number of years a bureaucratic mechanism in Scotland for thinking about these things and doing something about them. It is partly too the result of the excellent work that has been undertaken in Scottish universities, and here I must mention the work of Professor Donald Robertson in Glasgow and of my colleague Professor Johnson-Marshall. The projects planned and agreed and underway in Scotland account for a very large proportion of the present projected population increase in Scotland to the end of the century and this can hardly be said to be true anywhere else in the United Kingdom. Of course, it is an easier job in Scotland because the projected population increase in Scotland is a good deal smaller in percentage terms, than it is in other parts of the United Kingdom. Nevertheless, we are committed and perhaps over-committed to the end of the century, and we are committed to a much larger degree of population movement than is envisaged elsewhere in the country. This partly arises because of the extraordinary congestion in Glasgow and because of the narrowness of the belt of land suitable for settlement in the west of Scotland. But the Scottish National Plan implies that a large part of new settlements or resettlement in Scotland shall occur in the east of the Scottish central belt. There is the very considerable growth planned for the Livingston area, there are the plans for the growth of Dundee, there is the very large expansion going forward in the south Fife area, and there are points of new settlement elsewhere. There is, for example, the expansion in the Central Borders, necessarily a small one. There is the question of Aberdeen and its surrounding towns, which at present are under study by Professor Gaskin at Aberdeen, and there is the question of Inverness and the Moray Firth area.

How does this fit in with the issue of the role of big towns and small towns in urban growth? Dundee certainly fits in pretty well – it is the kind of large population centre that fits in best with the kind of economic framework discussed here. Livingston is somewhat less apposite. It is a somewhat anomalous creation, sufficiently large according to its plans to provide a considerable measure of self-support. On the other hand, it ranks as a satellite to Edinburgh with respect to the bulk of its services and cultural activities, and this is not an easy balance.

The development in south Fife requires a closer and more critical inspection. South Fife is a place that does attract industry, and the best kind of industry – growth industry, high wage industry, technological industry. It is a great success story. It fits in well with the point of view of some modern planning theorists, since it is the epitome of the nodal development; it consists of small communities linked together by good transport facilities. Each one of these nodal points is fairly small and has good access to the countryside. It is the kind of world which is very fashionable among planners today. On the other hand, we must ask ourselves whether in the long run in the competitive atmosphere of the 1980s and 1990s, in the struggle for the attraction of mobile industry, south Fife can hope on its present basis to continue its success. One wonders whether it has the labour market and the ancillary services to do this. One must ask too whether the dependence upon Edinburgh as a service and cultural centre really does make long-term sense for this area. This dependence upon Edinburgh depends upon easy communication. If we look at the bottleneck that is provided by the Forth Bridge, if we look at the pressure on the facilities in Edinburgh, then the present development in south Fife may not be as attractive as it seems. The question is thus raised whether we ought to reconsider the future development of south Fife and to think in terms of a large centre on the North side of the Forth, perhaps based on Kirkcaldy – perhaps expanding Kirkcaldy in the kind of doughnut previously described. Such a development would produce a chain of population centres down the east side of Scotland – Aberdeen, Dundee, greater Kirkcaldy and Edinburgh – a chain which would be extraordinarily attractive to industry and would attract a great deal of public investment, and especially investment in communications. Such a development might go a long way towards relieving the difficulties of Aberdeen. A more complete development in south Fife together with a development in Dundee would increase the economic viability of Aberdeen to an important degree. Aberdeen is just at that dangerous size, about 150,000 – 200,000, at which cities move from being commercially attractive to being commercially unattractive. One has the feeling that this critical size is creeping upwards so that while Aberdeen is not growing rapidly now it seems likely that it may begin to decline in population in the near future if no action is taken.

Discussion

SIR ROBERT MATTHEW
I want to go back to Professor Wolfe's point on green belts. This is one of these hunches that planners had in the days of Abercrombie and, for want of anything better, that hunch has (I think) performed a useful purpose – I do not think for a moment it had any economic basis but Abercrombie, and others who were thinking at that time, were simply giving a kind of insurance agains the future. They were saying that if towns continued to expand indefinitely there was going to be a very considerable deficit of open space, and therefore they should provide some sort of insurance belt. I do not believe it had any particular agricultural basis although you will find vague references to green belts. I think the basis of it was simply a hunch and like many of the planners' hunches of that time it was probably much better and more justified than they believed themselves; I think they did a good job.

There is one other point on green belts which Professor Wolfe did not refer to, and that was the existence of the character of topography. In Wellington, New Zealand, the surveyors who laid out the first town plan of Wellington, at least had a look at the topography and they decided they were not going to allow building up on the slopes, which have still been left as open space. The town has jumped right over the back, but I believe that nobody would ever argue nowadays that that should have been developed. There is also a thing called the 'Matthew Stop Line' in Belfast right now which was there for very much the same reason.

Dr Stone is one of the few men who have been working in this field over the last few years and it has always surprised me that the government and the public authorities responsible for large-scale development have not got into this field very much earlier. I do not believe that when the first range of New Towns came to be decided there was any great costing at all. I would like Dr Stone to comment on this; indeed I am not sure that even when it came to the Mark 3-that is the Cumbernauld range – that there has been any extensive costing. The reasons that led to developing the New Towns were of quite different order and I am not sure that many basic decisions taken on urban planning had any great economic basis at all. Politicians are not generally economic animals, they are highly emotional animals and most of the decisions are taken for quite other reasons. I would certainly agree that when it comes to areas of choice between alternatives if some techniques of estimating costs and benefits could be developed then so much the better.

What sort of comparative costs studies were made for the development of the new universities? I imagine that the provision of new university places has been done in the most expensive way you could possibly do it. (I speak in a very ambivalent way of this because my own office is designing five new universities; I am also a member of this university which is caught short of funds to a most alarming degree.) I do not think for a moment any relative cost studies were made and the first question I have to ask Dr Stone is 'What is the reason?' When architects design individual buildings, in almost every sphere now, in hospitals, in universities and houses, we are cost planned almost out of existence. Cost planning has got to such an extreme stage that it is almost impossible to plan a building nowadays. But cost planning on a larger scale is almost entirely missing and the question is 'What is the reason for that great difference in attitude to cost planning?'

When we come to standards, this seems to me to be a basic consideration in almost everything. When we look over, even glance superficially at, the range of standards that are applicable in some way or other to the built environment, we get a most extraordinary picture. Dr Stone has said that too few of the standards commonly used in urban planning appear to have any firm basis and I agree with him. It depends of course on what he means by 'firm'. A whole host of standards have an extraordinary precise basis, probably much too precise. When you look at the origin of many of the standards, they go back to basic considerations of public health, structural safety, and various things of that kind; in the field of housing the standards are fantastically precise, but the basis on which they are made is highly questionable. On other aspects of the built environment, standards are vague and on a still larger sector, they are non-existent. Professor Colin Buchanan is constantly saying that the standards in relation to environment and the separation of transport from environmental areas are entirely baseless as far as any standards are concerned. Therefore my second question would be 'How does Dr Stone see this question of bringing together standards over the whole range of the environment in some sort of coherent system? Is there any likelihood of this taking place or are we likely to continue for many years, working on this extraordinary patchwork of irrational standards?

That leads me to a more precise aspect of standards. We are still very largely building in the way we have always built and the question is, 'In view of changing social habits and so on, is our length of life of buildings still far too long?' As far as I know the loan period of housing is still some sixty years, still almost what it was. Should that kind of thing now be in question? We come up a very real difficulty here. You can build houses for a much shorter period but I doubt if you can build roads. Once you put down roads they are extraordinarily durable, but here is a field that I think we ought to look at rather closely. That leads to my final point on durability and flexibility which are mixed up together.

We now get the view that we have been designing, not just single buildings, but whole communities on a much too rigid and inflexible basis and the alternatives that are being put forward at the moment are not very congenial to me as an old-fashioned architect. I think that these communities must be thought of very largely, in an open-ended way, and this of course tends to lead to indeterminacy, and I would have thought, loss of character. In that connection one is getting to the stage of planning for the future which never arrives and therefore never planning for current conditions. This I believe is one of the basic problems we have to think of when we are gathering all these factors together.

Finally when we come to the question of measuring standards, the earlier standards of a century or so ago I believe advanced the science of measurement. There are now many areas of what Dr Stone has called values, in which we have no great techniques for measurement but – and I would like him to expand a little on this – in which directions are we going? I think he is suggesting we ought to find out more what the community thinks about what they need. Is this not however in fact simply saying that we go at the rate of the slowest horse and is that itself not an inhibiting factor which would replace the hunches of the earlier planners – hunches which may be right and may be wrong but were occasionally imaginative.

C. BLAKE
I have one or two points I would like to make about Dr Stone's paper.

I think that this question of standards and what an economist might say about them is very interesting. It is not a technical problem of measuring and defining a standard but rather an economic problem; it is for example, a problem of how you set standards in such a way as to reconcile the capacity of the construction industry to deliver the goods and the willingness of the community to forgo alternative opportunities of resource allocation. I think I see, in Dr Stone's paper a tendency to assume that in a sophisticated society these standards must be set by administrative decision almost paternalistically. I do not hold the view myself. Here is after all something which traditionally, market forces are supposed to have done for us. However, I do accept it is still a widely held and still probably respectable view that there are many areas where building standards and general standards of urban life are fixed administratively even although it would be possible but not necessarily desirable to loosen up the operation of market forces to some extent. This could be achieved in the way in which we organize housing finance for example. There is a limited scope for getting round the difficulty of settling administrative standards, but there is still a large area where the government has to make decisions which relate the supply of construction and other resources to the community's requirements. How does one in fact set about measuring the community's requirements, its valuation of housing and other urban services.

I think here that a great deal can be done by techniques which I understand are now being developed, particularly with regard to transport by some of the economists now working at the Ministry of Transport. I think it is possible to do a great deal more than has been realised and I think this may be what Dr Stone had in mind about direct measurement from observed behaviour in quasi price situations. Here the attempt is to measure what in fact the consumer does want and how much in real terms he is prepared to pay, i.e. to forgo in other forms to get this standard of urban amenity or housing service. All that, of course, has to do basically with the economic problem of allocating resources between construction industry and other industries.

I turn now to the allocation of resources between new construction and repair and maintenance. I think this is really a quite fascinating question and one which industrial economists have largely ignored. How inefficient is the repair and maintenance sector of the construction industry? Quite apart from the regional differences which Dr Stone mentions in stocks of existing housing and in the labour force available for construction, there are other interesting regional differences. In the productivity of labour in construction there are interesting, and so far as I can discover, inexplicable differences in the regional allocation of construction work between new construction and repair and maintenance when this is measured in terms of the labour employed. In England and Wales it would appear that repair and maintenance in the short run has recently borne a fairly stable proportional relationship to the volume of new construction; this has not been so in Scotland where the relationship has been very unstable and would appear to suggest that repair and maintenance is falling very much faster as a proportion of the total than for the whole of the U.K.

This is a point reinforced in my mind by something Sir Robert Matthew said about the durability of the houses we are now building.

EC F

There must obviously be a very subtle interconnection between the volume of repair and maintenance work which is going to be required in the future (where that includes the improvement of the housing stock as it is today) and the volume of repair and maintenance work which is going to be made necessary by the housing stock we are building from today on. There is possibly scope here for the application of dynamic programming techniques where you get some quite interesting interplays between decisions you take today and what happens in the next stage.

The real thought that is in my mind is whether we are in the long run going to have to think of a distinction between repair and maintenance on the one hand and new construction with a large body of repair and maintenance work on the other? One possible conclusion of this is the disposable house, so that repair and maintenance as we now understand it becomes a very small, indeed insignificant part of the construction industry?

These are two points which are suggested to me by my own thinking about the Tayside problem. I am a cost benefit enthusiast where it can be applied but I am not nearly so sanguine as I think Professor Wolfe is about the possibilities of doing cost benefit studies on the merits of different conurbation patterns. Let us take as a particular case the choice between developing an existing urban area or building new small satellite or independent settlement in the area.

I think that when you take into account even the points Professor Wolfe specified – that in the various locational considerations that surround the siting of new and existing industries, the internal costs and external effects of each separate firm, the basic transport network interactions, the interaction between length of journey and congestion and the provision of main services – these alone, not to mention a lot of other factors one ought to bring in, make what seems to me in combination, an extremely difficult sum to solve. I think even to talk rather blandly about the use of computerized simulation models of these various cost interactions is only saying that this is a difficult problem and not really telling you how to solve it; it is one we certainly ought to take very seriously.

I am not as yet happy about our professional skill or competence as economists to produce the solutions that on paper we ought to be able to produce.

One last point on what I call the big city alternatives. Professor Wolfe made the point that if you are going to offer an alternative – even if it is a Hobson's Choice alternative to industries which have now located in the 'coffin belt' – you must offer them a large developed industrial city to go to. This I think may sometimes not even be arguing the matter far enough. One of the by-products of another study in Dundee would seem to suggest that there are a surprising number of industries for whom even the Glasgow West of Scotland area is not a big enough industrial complex for them to operate in efficient competition with their opposite numbers in say Birmingham, Manchester or London. These are industries which are heavily dependent on sub-contracting facilities, heavily dependent on finding people who will buy their scrap or their by-products and there is really only one possible location in the United Kingdom, and that is already almost pre-ordained.

GENERAL DISCUSSION

Emrys Jones. Two very brief points, on the implications of population movements. I think we should concentrate on the kind of population that moves. Between the wars for example, Wales lost 400,000 by migration; of these 400,000 eight per cent were males between the ages of sixteen and forty. It is the kind of population that is left behind that is the worry because within any population the number contributing to the economy is only a proportion. If one loses this proportion, this results in one of the major social problems.

The second point that I have to ask from Dr Stone's paper – Sir Robert Matthew has already referred to this – concerns the age of buildings generally and more specifically the age of office buildings. This is being controlled more and more by the age of the machinery that goes into them. I think the average age in London now is fifty years, while in New York it has reduced to twenty-five. Twenty-five years is the limit of air conditioning plant. We have to look at the position where the sheer mechanics of the thing would control the age of housing. How far does this affect Dr Stone's calculation of replacement housing in the next forty years?

D. White. My first question is a general one about market forces.

As a Civil Engineer my way of seeing a market force is in the literal sense of a market, where something is offered for sale and other people bid to buy – in other words there is an element of option. If the person offers a thing at a price and cannot sell it at that price, he has to reduce it. If the buyer does not want to pay he goes along to the next stall in the market. I cannot see that this has any relevance at all to the question of road prices and certain other things that Professor Wolfe mentioned in connection with the direction of industry. If you put an arbitrary price on a toll for instance you cannot offer several alternative routes to motorists at option. You cannot offer them the choice of paying so much per mile to go one way rather than another. You are not really, in my view, assessing the economic demand of the user of the road at all, you are imposing a form of control. It is a hidden control, it is an economic control, a form of direction which I thought emerged from Professor Wolfe's remarks in connection with industry and all the various kinds of taxes which are used to direct industries. Taxes are a form of fiscal control, not of putting out an option, except in so far as he mentioned this might be done with the Industrial Development Certificates. The question in this particular context in which these tolls on roads are really market values or are they forms of control?

Professor Matthew mentioned the Buchanan report and the laying down of standards for the kind of environment which we must define. One can define levels of noise, levels of fumes, levels of safety for instance but I would like to ask Sir Robert Matthew or Dr Stone whether we might finish up by defining environment in terms of those identifiable things and perhaps miss some of the non-identifiable things which constitute the environment.

Professor Matthew also mentioned that roads are built to last a long time. We are still working on the roads the Romans laid down, but road construction is of course very expensive and consequently once it is put down, we are stuck with it for many years to come. The engineer can cheat a little bit in a manner known as stage construction. We can of course only make guesses and predictions and estimates about the future but we can in fact design the minimum required for the moment. What must be done is to make provision for successors to build on the thing. For instance, take the very simple case of a roundabout. One can design a roundabout as a preliminary step but make provision so that an overpass or an underpass, as the case may be, can be built by successors. There is no need to make a massive investment at the beginning which might in fact turn out later on to be uneconomic if the concomitant developments of industry and housing do not take place.

To quote an example, a very large bridge has recently been designed with a dual two-way carriageway with cycle tracks. Of course no one wants cycle-tracks nowadays but as they are still mentioned in official literature, we put in cycle tracks. But the structural engineer designs those cycle tracks very carefully so that if in twenty years time the bridge proves inadequate, the cycle tracks may be converted to carriageways to carry motor traffic very simply and very cheaply. In the meantime we can get permission and grants for a dual two-way carriageway; if you wanted a dual three-way carriageway now, the job would not be done at all. So the highway engineer has in fact a little more flexibility than might appear to be the case.

W. Harris. Many people in local government feel frustration at the paucity of research into the efforts of the vast government expenditures which represent an attempt to solve the Development Area problem. I reckon that probably one hundred million pounds a year is the cost of implementing the Development Area policy as far as an area like the north-east of England is concerned. I cannot imagine any commercial undertaking spending one hundred million pounds a year on any particular product without doing at least a few hundred thousand pounds worth of research and development to find out what was going to happen for its money. As far as I have been able to find out, it is not a question of say five per cent of the annual cost being spent on research and development to find out the effectiveness of this expenditure. It is not even one half of one hundredth of one per cent. It seems to have been directed basically on a sort of political hunch and it is rather sad that everybody should talk about the techniques that are available for solving these problems and point out how well developed these are, yet nobody actually does it when it comes down to the point.

Coventry, in quite a different field, have recently had their policy studied by an operational research organization and they have come up with an ingenious idea although I do not know how well it could be made to work or whether even the necessary credibility could be established for it. Basically the idea consists of trying to get the politicians who have to make the judgements between the alternatives, to standardize their concept of what they consider to be a unit of political penalty. From there, the politicians try to express the disadvantages of alternative decisions in these terms. One of the units of political penalty would be putting up rents for example.

Another of the points is the question of housing. People might be interested to know of two or three things that are happening in Newcastle. We have a very extensive housing programme that is planned to go on to the mid-80s, and possibly beyond the year 2000. We have run into problems of conflict between the results we achieve in the long run and our immediate requirements. We want to get houses in the long term, we also want houses in the short term. We also want high standards throughout the long term but we are having difficulty in implementing these in the short term. We do not want to disrupt communities unnecessarily but for physical reasons we are finding we have to. We want houses in different places in the short term from where we would put them in the long term. We are in fact establishing at the moment a mathematical model of this whole system. This model takes account of the problem of not only maintaining old houses, but of improving old houses so that they are at least equal to the current standards of Parker-Morris. Some of them of course will be substantially better in terms of actual space. Not only are we bringing them into good repair but we intend to repair them so that they will last for forty years by giving them all that new houses require in terms of facilities. This will greatly reduce the maintenance required in the intervening period. Also we are dealing with them not one by one or in clusters but as an essential part of the District and Action Area plans that we are developing. This is part of the total town planning procedure in the city and is something they are attempting to solve by dynamic programming.

The efficiency with which the maintenance work is being done is worth mentioning. Our experience at the moment is that you can spend anything up to £2,500 a house in addition to the acquisition cost. We still think that it is good value for money because you can preserve the social capital, without a tremendous amount of upheaval. This of course includes the environmental work that has to be done to go along with it. I think it is an inefficient use of resources to improve houses without improving the environment which is a relatively small part of the total cost.

Sir Robert Matthew referred to the way in which the technicians and architects and civil engineers construct things in this day and age. When you have a rapidly advancing technology at an accelerating rate, it is sheer stupidity to lock current techniques, and social habits, into a form where it is bound to remain concrete for something like a hundred years. It was encouraging to hear Sir Robert say that the architectural profession, and presumably those professions which serve it, can make houses that will only last for a much shorter time presumably at the same equivalent annual cost. I do not know whether whole cities would be subject to the same sort of approach if this were pursued. I think this will have to come eventually and certainly where you are under stresses of the sort we are going to be under in terms of population during the next hundred years, we will have to follow techniques something like those which were followed in laying down temporary airstrips and so on during war time.

Sir Robert Matthew. On the question of location of industry I think Professor Wolfe was arguing that they needed large centres. I think we have to remember three particular aspects of industry. Firstly industry is not a monolithic block of human activity that has general characteristics – it is very far from it in that some industrialists will do one thing and some another. I would remind you that in Austria in the last few years industrial firms like Good Year, Enkalon and Kenstrachen have all settled there with very large plants and in very small communities. Secondly industrialists are human beings and many of them have got wives and dependents whose views sometimes have a determining factor in where they are going to go. Thirdly with regard to Scotland, if one looks at three different blocks of industry, one observes that power stations are not at all dependent on location in relation to large towns; the tourist industry is generally not connected with the large towns and neither is the construction industry itself. One of the most progressive builders in Scotland is centred in the very small village of Muir of Ord, very far from the central belt. So if we are thinking of location of industry in relation to the size of communities I think we have to be very careful we do not fall into the trap of thinking that industry belongs to one category only.

P. Stone. Professor Matthew asked about cost planning. I do not really know why little cost planning was done in new towns. I do not think much cost planning was done in buildings fifteen to twenty years ago when the first new towns were developed. I think this is only gradually progressing.

Much more important I think is the question raised about standards. What I have in mind here is that of the many standards which are suggested, some are laid down very firmly for development, in terms of absolutes. I think most of them are really relatives. For example, we have established standards for amounts of daylight, sound transmission and so on although we do not have any standards relating much to noise. I think we have really to try and look at the whole range of standards and try and determine the relative values people attach to these factors. It may well be that people would much prefer for example to have environment much freer from noise even if they had to sacrifice some other standard to it. I think we have to try and look at standards as a whole and find out what are the relative weights people give to them; also to try and see which is the combination which really gives them the most satisfaction.

On the question of durability, the difficulty I find here is that while I think we can produce buildings which are less durable than the ones we are generally using, can we produce buildings with a short durability which are cheaper in the long run? I think Mr Harris had the point when he said 'at the same annual cost'. As far as I can see we cannot do this and if we were to put up buildings to last say for twenty years then the annual cost would probably be about sixty per cent more than those of the normal life today. The idea of disposal units has been suggested. Again as far as technology goes at the moment we cannot really think in terms of having disposable units of buildings. We might however think in terms of having disposable components within buildings. We are certainly getting components in buildings these days, and the actual cost of the shell of the building itself is becoming of declining importance. I think the cheapest form of flexibility and adaptability in buildings is probably space, because the costs do not rise anything like in proportion to the increase in space. Given a fairly adequate amount of space to start with, you can adapt a building fairly easily when the need arises.

The problem one is put against in this question of adaptability in the life of both buildings and developments is this limit on resources which, as I indicated in my paper, seems to be serious. We are going to have some difficulty, unless we can find much more in the way of resources, to replace dwellings which are already over eighty years old by the end of the century.

On this question of market forces I agree with Professor White that if the prices for things like tolls and road prices were fixed rigidly once and for all then they would not give us very much indication of demand; if they were allowed to fluctuate according to demand then one could eventually find out what the going price for this sort of facility was. If the going price was high enough, there would be an indication that more of that sort of facility should be provided.

Finally, I will refer to one or two remarks that Professor Wolfe raised about work which we are doing at the Institute on Costs. So far we have only looked at the capital costs, though we have also done the journey to work costs. It took this form because of what the Ministry was prepared to pay for, but we are hoping to go on to look at operation costs; these are things like the costs of journeys to work and all the other sort of costs – the costs of local government services, the cost of firms in towns of different sizes, different forms and so on. I think there is some possibility that we will make fairly rapid advances in this. There is always the question of values on which we would also like to get some results but I think this is a very much more difficult problem. Certainly the differences which we have found in the cost of construction with the different forms and sizes of towns are not considerable.

There are really two major factors. First of all, density, in whatever form it comes does add substantially to the cost of development. Most other things seem to affect the cost through the road system and the increase in costs by increasing town size seem to be fairly small. But it is not just the cost of the road system it is also for example the cost of the journeys to work; these rise fairly substantially as you increase the size of the town and they are quite important. I think one of the myths about town development is this question of economy of scale. Now we have not found really any economy of scale over the sort of range we have been looking which has been fifty to two hundred and fifty thousand. Certainly, at the bottom and below this level there is some evidence of economy of scale taken for public utility services and in some of the other facilities. But over this range there does not seem to be any economy of scale. A regional Gas Board and a regional Electricity Board actually costed their services out for us on a series of models over this size range and they found no significant economies of scale.

I think what is perhaps the most important thing that has come out of these studies to date, is the effect of the costs of the expansion of towns as compared with green field towns. Here the differences can be very substantial but this really depends on the way in which a town is expanded. The method suggested earlier was to take an existing town and to blow it up into a much larger one. This usually involves redeveloping the town centre and destroying a great number of facilities which have a fairly considerable value. The amount of redevelopment can be reduced considerably, depending on the type of town centre and general development which exists. For example, if you develop on what is normally known as a district centre type of town where each district has a large amount of its services in the main town centre, this centre tends to be fairly confined and obviously reduces the amount of demolition work which has to be done. Hence costs are reduced both of demolishing buildings which have got a sound life and of redeveloping on land which has previously been developed. The other technique which can produce even lower costs is actually to build a series of other towns to form some sort of cluster around the existing town. Perhaps in fact eventually one of these other towns could be made the main centre, so that the amount of redevelopment which you actually incur for the existing town is similar to the normal renewal process required to bring the Town up to the standards and requirements of the next twenty or thirty years.

J. N. Wolfe. Dr Blake expressed his pessimism about research in this field. It is really rather hard to believe that vastly increased sums of research and development on the underlying economic problems would not be appropriate, no matter how difficult the problems may be. Certainly it is amazing how much you can do with economic problems if you work on them and spend a little money on them. The revolution in the economics of defence that has occurred in the United States in the past fifteen years under the impact of such people as Hitch and Endhoven is important. We tend to run behind the United States in these matters but the United States is fortunately beginning to worry about her urban affairs and a great scientific spin off will no doubt begin soon. However I really think it is wrong to wait until somebody else does this kind of thing when you think how very much more this kind of work has been done on a consciously planned basis in this country and how little research has supported it.

In conclusion, I think we will be moving towards a period within a very few years when the housing programme will be cut back. The resources will be released for the kind of factory and infra-structure building on which the prosperity of the country depends. There will also be a much increased programme of repair and maintenance in old buildings. The recent White Paper on New Houses out of Old is one of the most encouraging developments that could have occurred in the whole field of public expenditure.

The Approach of an Economist-Errant

J. PARRY LEWIS

I must begin with an explanatory apology. When I agreed to give a lecture at the Edinburgh Conference I did so on condition that there was no need to put anything on paper until later in the summer. A couple of days before I was due to speak I went down with laryngitis, and the organizers were left with neither speaker nor paper. Into the breach sailed Professor Wolfe, and the field of urban studies is enriched by this forced application of his powerful mind to a subject which economists for so long ignored. He and Dr Stone have at least touched on most of the points I would have made. To avoid repetition, or a controversy which would give me an unfair advantage unless we ran into Replies and Rejoinders, I am going to dwell upon a few points which are rather more general, and more concerned with methodology, than those which I would originally have made the basis of my contribution. Whether they are 'economic' points depends on how you define the subject. But they *are* points which occur to me because I am an economist, wandering (in only one sense, I hope) in another field.

The first is the simple concept of opportunity cost. When we look at urban growth from this standpoint we see at least three things which the town-planner and urban administrator must keep in mind. One is that bricks, labour and money which are used to create buildings of certain kinds in certain places cannot at the same time be used in other ways. Since all of these may at any moment be scarce, the planner (or urban decision-taker) has to choose the way in which his resources will be used. Once he has used them he provides the town with a stream of services which will last for several years. He also generates a stream of problems, as buildings generate traffic, waste disposal needs, and so on. A different use of the resources would have led to a different stream of services and of problems. The idea of discounted cash flow can be used to compare these streams, provided that one can find suitable discount rates and ways of measuring the services and nuisances created. Monetary valuation may not be necessary, if quantitative comparisons can be made. If all of this can be done, and it is a big 'if', then the opportunity cost of a proposed allocation of resources can be determined, and decision can be better informed.

But, and this brings me to the second application of this concept, one of the resources is land, to which is inevitably associated location. When a piece of land is used for a particular purpose it means not only that that land cannot be used for something else, but also that the uses of land round about are affected : and this is part of the opportunity cost of that land-use. Here we are immediately up against a whole chain of consequences, for a decision to use one plot in a certain way may first affect the uses to which adjacent plots are put, and so the uses to which more remote plots (adjacent to these) are put, and so on. It is a chain of consequences which every planner tries to foresee : but usually it extends, like a game of chess, beyond the few immediate possibilities which the imagination and logic of the decision taker can produce.

The third application of this simple statement of the opportunity cost concept is temporal rather than spatial. In any town there is a whole host of things to be done. The order in which they are done may be important. If resources are likely to become available in more or less equal quantities every year, then action X taken now may enable action Y to be undertaken more cheaply next year : whereas Y now would leave the cost of X next year unaffected. Considerations of this kind should properly figure in decision-taking. If it happens that resources are likely to be available unevenly over time, or that needs are likely to arise unevenly, then it may be more important than ever to do so.

It is worth mentioning a couple of examples of this last point. If one is building a new town should one provide shops and recreation facilities in advance of the bulk of the housing, or only when an adequate population has already been housed ? The point here is that if one is seeking to attract industry to a new area the non-existence of these services may deter some of the key-workers from moving and so lead to the non-arrival of industry, and so to the existence of empty factories and houses. It is a matter which was important at Dawley, where it had substantial cost implications.

A second example is with us almost everywhere today. There is need to provide additional houses. There is also need to renew. In the early seventies the former need will temporarily decline. How should building and renewal programmes be framed in order to make most use of this ?

These examples and my invocation of opportunity cost have set up a number of questions which I have not attempted to answer. But I think that they have also underlined two facts. One is the complexity of the consequences of urban decisions. The other is the need to measure, if rational decision-taking is to be well-informed. I want to justify the use of the word 'need' because it is a much over-used word, and should, in my opinion, always be uttered in the context of a purpose. Our housing 'need', for example, depends on the standards we care to adopt, and our aim about the achievement of those standards.

At a rough calculation, which may well be 20 per cent out, urban investment in Western countries is now running at a per capita rate of about £120 per annum. This is based on data for sixteen countries with a total population of 500 million people, and represents a total urban expenditure in these countries by £600,000 million. If, by some means or the other, we could reduce this sum by 3 per cent and obtain a not-inferior stream of services from it, then we would be liberating £18,000 million worth of resources. If our aim is to use our resources efficiently then there is need of an approach which can indicate what decisions will lead to more 'economic' or 'efficient' outcomes. Yet, as I have indicated, attempts to do this lead us to questions which are far from easy to answer.

Few towns now grow as fast, in percentage terms, as many did in the nineteenth century; but in absolute terms there is often growth on an unprecedented scale. We have more towns than ever before; they are larger; and they are growing rapidly. Simply as a consequence of size, a number of problems arise. The number of potential trips within a town is, after all, proportional to the square of the number of people in it. This, in itself, is one reason why the rate of growth of problems may exceed the rate of growth of towns. But, quite apart from this, there are technological changes and new levels of income which generate further problems. Many stem from the increase in car ownership, which rests on both of these. On the other hand, the prophets of gloom must not have it all their own way. I wonder to what extent the load on our roads, especially at night, has been reduced by the invention of television? There may well be other inventions which, in unexpected ways, may reduce rather than increase the number or scale of problems we have to face.

But I digress. The point I really want to make is that because of rapid growth, the number of sizable towns, the need to renew, and the continuing revolution in transport and communications, we are today faced with urban problems more complex than ever before, with investment exceeding levels previously contemplated, and with the need to solve these problems in a way which makes this investment more efficient. Unwittingly we may be designing a town which will be slightly cheaper to build but much less efficient in operation; or attempting to solve a traffic problem by a policy which leads to empty shops and urban decay. The town has to be considered as an expanding entity in a wider context; and it has to be recognized that all the parts of this entity interact in a way which we have hardly begun to measure, and only inadequately understood. We are asking our designers and decision-takers to act without knowing enough about the consequences of their actions.

In its complexity and need of measurement, urban decision-taking is much like economic decision-taking : but its theory is less advanced and, in my view, its complexities are greater, partly because of the location factor. I think that the economist is, by his basic training, well equipped to tackle many of these problems, once he has got hold of a feeling for space (which takes longer than some people think). He is not trained to feel for space, to synthesize a range of conflicting requirements into a workable solution, or to design. He is trained to ask about chains of consequences and remote effects; to tackle problems involving allocation decisions; to think of time-lags and delayed reactions; to think at different levels of aggregation and reality; to build models and to measure.

There was a time when intuition, a feel for things, a set of analytical maps and some broad quantifications could produce a town plan which stood a good chance of solving more problems than it created. The same kind of approach was useful in taking decisions about traffic, refuse-disposal and other urban operations. As towns have grown the inadequacies of these methods have become more apparent and planners have been the first to point out that they need better tools than they have. Just as the carpenter uses a saw, and says what job it must do, but does not make one, so the planner is saying that he needs the help of other disciplines in providing him with tools to do particular jobs. And he goes further, by saying that sometimes he wants to sub-contract those jobs to the men who make the tools.

The power of economic analysis as a planning tool, and of the application of economic theory as a means of control, has been demonstrated by Professor Wolfe; and I shall not consider it further. But one of the things we have learned in economics is the use of behavioural hypotheses, and of measurement.

In the field of urban planning and administration there are lamentably few quantified hypotheses, and even less measurement of a kind that may help to test them, or to quantify relationships. Most of what does exist concerns traffic : but even this is often blinkered, in the sense that often only part of the story is considered.

One set of hypotheses has become well known coming under the heading of 'the gravity model', which states, in general terms, that N opportunities (to work, to shop, or to engage in any other activity) located at a distance d will exert an 'attraction' proportional to N^α / d^β; and that this attraction will be reflected in the way a group of people divide their activities between various centres, according to their 'size' (N) and distance (d). Following the derivation of gravitational laws in statistical mechanics, Alan Wilson has shown that this formula can be derived from a set of behavioural assumptions : but one of these implies that a change in the price of a mode of transportation will leave total expenditure on transportation unchanged – which does not seem to be supported in fact. Even so, it may well be possible to derive the formula from a different set of assumptions.

This particular 'model' has been used with varying degrees of realism. Sometimes it has been assumed that $\beta = 1$, and empirical observations have then enabled α to be calculated. When no such assumption has been made, and observations have preceded estimates of both α and β, it has often been found that β is significantly different from zero : and that, as might be expected, its value varies from activity to activity.

But a question that is rarely asked is one which is akin to the identification problem of econometrics. Just as price statistics reflect the outcome of the demand schedule and the supply schedule, so information about, for example, the distances from various work opportunities at which people live will reflect the outcome not only of how jobs attract settlement of people, but also of how centres of population attract jobs : and until this is built into the model its use to predict how people will react (in settlement terms) to a new location of employment is likely to be misleading.

I have spoken in particular about this model partly because it is so widely misused, but also because it illustrates the dangers that arise from three different sources. One is the tendency to carry over into urban studies theories and methods which were devised for other fields. (Another example is the indiscriminate use of ordinary correlation analysis on geographical variables, disregarding the effects of proximity.) The second source of potential trouble is the desire to simplify and to aggregate, without adequate consideration of the conditions under which it is right to do this. The third source is the tendency to believe that patterns of settlement and activity which (even today) are still currently determined more by what went on before 1939 than after 1945 will continue to reveal information that will be useful in designing for 2000. I do not suggest that these approaches must always, or even usually, lead to wrong results.

All of this is but a paraphrase of part of the dilemma that faces the econometrician; and I may seem to be guilty of crime myself, carrying over into urban studies too much that has been devised for the economist. But I hasten to assert that I have merely indicated problems and dangers. I have not yet proposed solutions.

It is time to do so : and I begin by emphasizing that long before
computers were invented, planners and legislators were, in effect and
sometimes very deliberately, setting up simple behavioural models,
and using them to help reach a decision. The computer revolution
enables faster and more realistic models to be built. Some are good :
some bad. What matters is that they provide a new possibility in the
study of towns; and in the design of tools for planners.

Here I want to make it clear that I am not advocating the use of
computer models to produce plans. I know that some people have
different ideas about this, but I think that a word of caution is necessary. So far as I know, computer-produced plans generate landuse
patterns based on one of two approaches. One is an attempt to
optimize some function subject to certain constraints. As any
operational research man will know, the answer in a case like this can
be most illuminating, but often what it illuminates is the inadequacy
of the specification of the constraints, and the over-simplified nature
of the function to be optimised. Furthermore, if we tinker with the
solution we may quickly go right off the rails – as far as optimization
goes. Until planners can specify their objective in precise, quantifiable and addable units, optimization models will (if used automatically) remove from planning all that cannot yet be quantified;
while (if their results are modified by intuition) they will offer no
guarantee that a plan reached entirely by intuition would not have
been better.

The other kind of computer plan is based on such assumptions as
how people gravitate to various opportunities, under certain constraints. To some extent my remarks about gravity models are relevant here. But a major question which needs answering is : 'Should
plans be influenced by how people would act if there were no
planning?'

My personal view is that models are most useful to planners when
they allow him to predict the consequences of his proposed policies.
Essentially, this calls for the construction of simulation models, in
which the various components of urban activity are related to each
other. In theory, one can set up a model which spells out a 'description' of the town at specified moments, showing how the town ticks;
and if a new policy is contemplated this ticking of the town may
change, and the model enables us to follow the changes.

Work in this field is proceeding rapidly: but it must always rest
on empirical observation, and detailed studies of urban behaviour :
Under specified circumstances, what degree of parking restriction

can a suburban hardware store experience before there is a ten per cent fall in sales? How long will a certain kind of shopkeeper remain in business when sales are below past levels? How do developers decide on asking rents for shops, and offices? What factors influence the decision of where to shop, and what is the strength of the influence? These are but a few of the questions which need precise statement and empirical investigation if we are to build up a quantified knowledge of urban processes, of a kind that will help us to understand urban growth more precisely. When this has been done then we can experiment with policies in the computer rather than on the ground.*

In this short paper I have seemingly wandered a long way. Let me try to add some purpose to my journey. I began by talking of such things as opportunity-cost, of comparing one set of discounted flows with another, of the problems of land-use decisions setting up chain reactions, and so on. I also asserted the importance of being more efficient in our urban investment. The modern tendency is to invoke computer aids. Without adequate understanding of both towns and models this can be more damaging than useful. But we do have the opportunity to spell out the consequences of policies, over space and time, in a way which will allow us to compare policies, and so to know more about the choice that is before us. We can be better informed about the opportunity cost. To get to that stage we need to embark on a large programme of urban analysis, and in particular of urban decisions – including quite mundane decisions. We need more hypothesis testing, and more measurement. In short, we need polimetrics : not for its own sake, but as a tool which may enable us to ensure the more efficient growth of our towns. And in this context 'efficiency' has room for the aesthetic, and for concepts which defy quantification. It must, if only because in the end even these can have their economic consequences.

* Many of these ideas are now under active discussion by an O.E.C.D. group of experts, whose report will eventually form interesting reading for those interested in these problems.

Part Three · Geography

Some Geographical Aspects of Urbanization

EMRYS JONES

In a recent paper called 'Two Aspects of Urbanization', John Fried-man went some way towards clarifying the social and physical com-ponents of this phenomenon. The former he would prefer to call the urban process, the sum total of changes in way of life, in values and in social structure which derive from man's divorce from primary activities and which have increased until they are now gradually becoming dominant in western societies. The latter concerns the more commonplace equation of urbanization with living in the large compact communities we call towns and cities. It is this aspect, concerning spatial differentiation, which has particularly interested geographers and given rise to a considerable amount of geographical literature. But although there has been a tendency to ignore many aspects of the process of urbanization, these are two faces of the same coin. Unless we are prepared to argue that social changes are the out-come of distinctive settlement forms then we must concern ourselves in the way in which settlement forms have reflected social changes – within certain technological limits – and how they may develop today and in the future as an expression of continuing change.

The geographer's contribution to urban studies has centred on the densely built up settlement called 'town'. In the past the distinctive-ness of the town has been based on such things as severance of some men's activities with food production and the soil : the focusing of exchange on some kind of market and the need for protection, for-merly often expressed in the building of a wall around the settlement. True the distinctions have sometimes seemed very blurred between villages and towns, particularly in origins and early development; but generally speaking there is no difficulty in recognizing the very tangible object of our study.

With few possible exceptions, throughout its history the town has been a discreet physical entity as well as a reflection of a particular way of life. The wall has characterized endless towns from Jericho to late nineteenth-century Paris, a symbol of separation and distinctive-ness in style of living and in values. More recently physical cohesion may have been more a function of the limits of a specialized service such as sewerage, water or electricity. But in one way or another a distinction has arisen between town and country, urban and rural. Urbanization in the physical sense has always meant the degree to which a society lives in one kind of settlement rather than the other – the percentage of the population living in towns. We assume, therefore, that increasing urbanization means more towns and / or bigger towns. [Though it is well to remember that by this definition, urbanization remains constant if the rural population increases at the same rate as the urban. It is differential growth which is the normal measure of urbanization.]

Physically the division between town and country, particularly in a country like Britain, has become very blurred. Suburbs have been with us for a very long time. Whereas these were previously compact appendages of towns – in the last century they took on a new significance. British towns grew at an unprecedented rate, but it was not this alone which blurred the edges. Rather it was the desire to escape from the towns which at the peak of industrialization reached the nadir of human environment : a desire first indulged in by the middle classes, but later shared by a steadily increasing number of the less affluent as new means of transport made possible that schism between workplace and home which is now the outstanding characteristic of all our towns and cities. Tied in with this was the idea explored most deeply by Ebenezer Howard – that the country was the ideal physical environment for man and that somehow we should mix town and country to produce the best conditions for living. Suburbs tried to create an illusion of country as near as possible to the city centre for people still tied to it by work and services. So the centrifugal – centripetal movements still took place within a fairly easily defined urban context.

In fact, *containment* was one of the main reactions to the increasing spread of cities which reached a peak in this country between the two world wars. After the publication of Abercrombie's plan for London, the concept of a green belt was generally accepted as a remedy for unorganized – and disorganized – sprawl. The green belt is the twentieth-century equivalent of the medieval wall and moat, and naturally carries with it all the disadvantages as well as the advantages of limitation. But in containing London, Abercrombie still envisaged some expansion in the form of satellites beyond the green belt. These turned out to be neat bundles of suburbia – though physically infinitely better organized – each of which had its own green belt. Physically it looks as if we have the problem well in hand. True the green belt is nibbled at – the wall is crumbling – but one of the major assumptions in city planning is still containment. The emphasis is on the discreteness of new settlements. Every new town plan is preceded by the designation of area, and this very line is as inviolate as any city wall, and could seriously hamper the development of radically new urban forms. Physically we are reluctant to leave the long tradition of the Western city, and implicit in this tradition is containment and the continued acceptance of an implied division between town and country. Even when containment has failed there is a tendency to accept the extension of bricks and mortar – i.e. of high density – as marking the spatial limit of a town, as, for example, in Fawcett's definition of a conurbation.

In fact one would have to be blind to reality to miss the evidence of expansion beyond this limit, particularly in the process of urbanization. Economic links, symbolized by the commuter, have extended the real dependence of outlying areas far beyond the physical limit of continuous built-up land. Pahl has shown very clearly how an apparently rural hinterland can be socially transformed. The clearest evidence of this, according to Pahl, is segregation of classes. Stamp's 'adventitious population' is rapidly taking over what is still, in a physical sense, rural. The people moving into and beyond this fringe are urbanites. Even more subtle is the diffusion of urban ideas and values to rural areas which are physically remote. In terms of population, these areas are thinly populated. Even in 1951, four out of five people in England and Wales lived in towns. The fact that in 1961 the figure was the same indicates nothing more than that urban boundaries have not been changed to accommodate urban growth. Accretion has certainly been suburban, and already in a physical sense probably nine out of ten people live in towns. But in a social sense this country is rapidly becoming a hundred per cent urban, for many aspects of the urban way of life are no longer spatially differentiated. Many of Webber's underlying concepts of urbanization are concerned with communications – which are by no means tied to physical links. Until recently communications meant the meeting point of routes and this, together with the physical significance of fair and market, is the basis of the centrifugal and centripetal forces which have underlain the model of the Western city until recently. There is now a bewildering freedom from spatial limitation. In Webber's terms, propinquity was once a necessary condition of urban life; it is no longer so, thanks to radio, telecommunication, TV. Taken literally this means that the concept of central place need no longer apply. The towns *can* be replaced by a 'non-place urban realm'. Indeed, it is claimed that certain specialist activities in our societies are already operating on this assumption and that as specialization increases, along with real wealth, education and leisure, more and more people will be freed from the necessity for living in the close physical contact which was previously the most obvious feature of our towns and cities.

This is largely in the realms of theory and so far it has applied to only a very small proportion of our population. Whatever influence this kind of process is having on the physical forms of towns, we must also remember that even with continuing growth and expansion it can only immediately affect a relatively small proportion of settlements. Whether we like it or not we have inherited towns and cities in which propinquity is a primary component.

Although gradually breaking down, schism between town and country in a physical sense exists and is colouring our entire thinking about the problems of planning new settlements. It is difficult to overcome a division which is as old as civilization. Although we may be aiming at obliterating the division – which is what we mean by complete urbanization – we still have to frame our discussions in existing physical terms. We are back with the problem of distinguishing one land use from another, and there are certain basic premises which, in our time, demand a non-urban component. In the recent past more particularly the arguments have assumed that the town is a threat to the countryside as a farming and productive area. Interwar suburban sprawl in particular raised visions of a country laid waste by bricks and concrete and of agriculture driven to the wall. To many it seemed that postwar expansion was only going to hasten this process. To a very large extent, the researches of Professor Wibberley and Dr Best at Wye College have invalidated these arguments. The latter has shown convincingly that less land is lost to agriculture to become urban now than in the interwar years. Between 1934 and 1939 about 50,000 acres a year in England and Wales ceased being agricultural land and were built upon. Between 1955 and 1965 the average was 33,500. Dr Peter Stone has calculated that we need only continue our present programme of about 375,000 new houses per annum to 2,000 to more than satisfy the demands of our increasing population. And at the present standards of postwar new towns (about 50 persons per acre) this means a turnover of 1,600,000 acres to urban land – again an average of about 40,000 per annum. This will no more than continue a trend which has been steady since 1900 and is by no means accelerating, and which, as the table shows, even in the year 2000, will mean that no more than 15·4 per cent of all land will be urban.

By itself this might seem a threat to food production, but the complement of this is Professor Wibberley's argument that the increase in

Table 1

	000,000 acres urban areas	% total land use
1900	2·0	5·4
1930	2·6	7·0
1940	3·2	8·6
1950	3·6	9·7
1960	4·0	10·8
1970	4·4	11·9
1980	4·9	13·2
1990	5·3	14·3
2000	5·7	15·4

agricultural productivity at 1·3 per cent per annum is more than compensating for this loss and, given our present dependence for some food on overseas sources, will continue to do so. Assuming selective urban expansion and continuing technical progress, Wibberley sees no threat in the present trend. The arguments are to a large extent irrelevant to the town versus country debate. In most general terms, the transfer of land to urban use need not necessarily affect our agricultural output in the near future – if we assume expansion at similar densities to our present standards. Even if our present average urban density is halved, the amount of land transferred will be increased only from 1·6 m. acres to 2·1 m. acres by 2000. But clearly much will depend on densities if we lower these greatly in the future.

The problems implicit in raising or lowering densities are relevant. It is quite clear that if Webber's assessment of the trends of urban process and urban expansion in the USA are correct, this is leading towards a gradual elimination of the distinctive high density urban settlement forms we have always been used to. Theoretically there is no reason why ultimately all settlement should not be completely dispersed. Los Angeles is often put forward as an example of a city where this process is already taking place, though in fact it ranks 18th in the 25 most densely populated urban areas (4,736 per sq. mile), above Boston and Miami. Perhaps Alberquerque or Las Vegas would be better examples. True, the population of the urbanized area of Los Angeles is nearly three times that of Boston, and that area is second in size only to New York – North-Eastern New Jersey. But its immense spread and increasingly very low densities are seen by some as a pointer to the future, particularly as these are related to ease of communication. Propinquity is loosening its grip. In our affluent society more people can afford the luxury of a larger or remote parcel of land without suffering the inconvenience which extreme scatter once implied.

In this country our concern with densities has long been coupled with the desire to improve the urban environment along the lines laid down by Ebenezer Howard. The idea of a standard of 12 houses or about 50 people to the acre has long been an established ideal, given the blessing of successive Ministries and adhered to by generations of planners. The New Towns Committee *Report* of 1946 actually recommended half this density, but in fact the average for all new towns in Britain, apart from Cumbernauld, is about 50 persons per acre. New towns are using relatively less land than the average turnover of agricultural land to urban uses in the last forty years : even so they are little more than contained pockets of what used to be derided as urban sprawl. In this respect planners and architects have tended to pull in opposite directions : whereas Best classifies new towns as moderate to high density, architects have been critical of their low density, of an 'extremity of wilderness' of 'prairie planning'. Best is scathing of the latter approach, quoting figures to show how mistaken they are, but in fact these critics are denouncing what they see – not a figure on paper. Maybe years of laburnum cultivation will soften the prairie : even so we have nothing better, nothing worse, than the interwar suburb. In fact, the words 'low', 'medium' and 'high' applied to density are meaningless except as statistical concepts. They are a measure. Unfortunately we have adopted them as a standard, and unwittingly equated all that is desirable in residential areas with low densities and all that is undesirable with high. When Best pleads that new town densities are too high he is pleading for 'more space to allow greater privacy', less noise, less congestion, better health and better amenities. This is begging the question; privacy, for example, does not necessarily result from having more space. Gardens both in new towns and in suburbs notoriously lack privacy : this is a function of how living space is planned, not how big it is. Noise, frequently cited as an undesirable concomitant of high density, could perhaps be better dealt with by insulation than by greater spacing of houses. To think that lower density is an answer to all our ills is a snare and a delusion. As a standard of environmental quality density is not very meaningful. My plea is not for high densities, but for the abandoning of the use of this concept as the main standard of a better residential environment.

Many of the desirable criteria of an adequate environment can be met within the limits of so called high density. A more critical need is to realize that different groups in society, particularly age groups, have different requirements. Perhaps the most elaborate provision for a complex situation is that suggested by Buchanan in his South Hampshire Study. Here he suggests six models of development and density, the latter ranging from 15 persons per acre to 130. He further assumes seven kinds of household structure, ranging from single to 5·5 per household with an age component. By setting these against one another he arrives at seven housing types from single-storey detached to 12-storey flats : these would be built in proportion to the projected classes of households by type of development. The gross density is that accepted in any new development.

The choices before us for urban expansion or for a new settlement are many. (1) An acceptance of present levels of residential density with the traditional emphasis on the two-storey house. No great concern would be occasioned by any threat to agricultural land because demands would be modest. The result would be a regulated suburbia. (2) A modest lowering of densities would modify, but not radically change, the picture as far as demands on land are concerned. (3) A sophisticated adjustment to social needs. The essence of this approach is the need for flexibility, so that a person could move easily to dwellings which would be adapted to different stages in the life cycle. The South Hampshire study is a sophisticated attempt which approaches this. Total demands on the land would be approximately what they are now. (4) A radical increase in net density, either as high density, low rise housing, tower blocks, or such experiments as Habitat '67. (5) A very radical lowering of densities along the lines suggested by suburban development in the USA, and towards the Webber concept; or controlled ribbon development as suggested by March. (6) A modification of the widely dispersed pattern by restricted high density nodes.

Even allowing for no radical innovations during the next thirty years or so, British society is going to change considerably. By the year 2000 the population of the UK will probably be about 75 million and the number of houses that will have been built between now and then, at present rates, will be about 15 million. But the quality of living will have changed also. Even by 1985, great changes can be foreseen. Cars will have increased by 130 per cent, the working day will be considerably shorter than it is today, real income will be doubled, the amount of time spent on education more than doubled. All these, incidentally, are a necessary part of the Webber hypothesis. Demands on the land are going to change. Perhaps bigger gardens for leisure activities will be one change. We know already, however, that other leisure activities are making larger demands in the public sector – for more recreation and sports grounds, parks and picnic areas; and there is a marked increase in the use of weekend cottages which can be reached only by car.

A massive increase in recreational demands on the countryside can be expected if present day trends continue. Affluence and increased mobility could turn the whole of Britain into a summer madness. The coasts, although far from saturated, are already generating a tedious pattern of lines of cars : for nowhere in Britain is more than about 70 miles from the sea. This pattern has only just begun to turn back on itself to explore the countryside. At the moment about 3 million acres are available for recreation in England and Wales, but the demand for more is imminent.

To some extent these activities are already being controlled. 10 per cent of the land area of England and Wales is in National Parks, another 5 per cent designated as areas of outstanding natural beauty. If green belts and their probable extensions are added, it means that a considerable percentage of the land area – possibly a third – must be strictly controlled. These are the areas which must form an important facet of future urban process in Britain even though they may exclude urban expansion. Nor must we forget that although agricultural productivity may balance a continuing decrease in agricultural land, much of agriculture itself may become so specialized and mechanized as to demand an exclusiveness which it hasn't had up to now. No weekenders would be tolerated casually crossing a factory floor, and it may well be that much of the farming of the future will demand the same protection. Certain kinds of activities could be met by multiple use of certain areas, but this, too, demands a positive planned approach rather than a haphazard overlapping which could lead to conflict. Indeed, apart from intensive farming, our approach to land use must be seen as complementary to the urban process, and it must be as firmly under control as urban sprawl. A rush of settlement could effectively destroy the value of recreational areas. It follows that town growth – or suburban growth – must be structured within these demands. Although theoretically the future population of this country could be thinly spread everywhere, in practice restriction is essential because of the kind of activities which are becoming so important in our society. The hypothetical half acre per person at the end of the century makes sense only if we are selective. For example, there is much to be said for living in very compact settlements during a working week if we are allowed the use of a cottage or caravan on the Welsh uplands during the weekend. There is even some value in calculating density not so much by the amount of land on which a house stands, but by the areas accessible to and used by households. In this respect, perhaps we should lean less towards the American pattern but examine the Scandinavian in more detail.

It is clear that the basic pattern of most urban settlement in Britain will not change for a long time. We have inherited so much urban stock that exciting changes could only be fringe activities in the very near future. And presumably we will have to wait for the development of the self-sufficient house before we can feel really free from urban services. The caravan has come very near to this ideal and is a strong indication of the way in which mobility can make nonsense of city boundaries : it forces us to think of the land use of the entire country when discussing urbanization.

The social assessment of the physical landscape is a strong element in the future settlement pattern. The concept of urbanization as a social process overrides physical constraint but, in turn, demands careful control over all land use before social aims can be realised to the best advantage. Urban – rural differences are being eroded because these two traditional aspects are being increasingly shared by more and more people. What kind of residential pattern develops outside our existing towns remains to be seen. Within the constraints we have noted there must be great flexibility, with ease of movement taking some kind of priority. But however much a dispersal of activities becomes a possibility, it will be difficult to gainsay the apparent desire of so many people to come together in large groups despite ease of communications. The desire for space may be matched with a desire for group activities. There is no reason why both should not be catered for. Mobility will enable everyone to share in different kinds of experience. It is with a feeling of dread that one envisages the logical conclusion of the freeing of urban society from those restraints which once enforced propinquity. Perhaps, after all, there will be fragments of Jane Jacob's city around the corner of every garden suburb of tomorrow.

Urbanization and Economic Development

H. BOWEN-JONES

In this paper I am speaking not as an urbanist but as a geographer, concerned with economic geography and particularly involved in the teaching, research and consultancy aspects of economic development mainly in the Middle East. I tend to regard towns as no more or less than normal elements in the landscape and I am vastly encouraged to find various lines of parallelism in what has already been said and in what I propose to say.

It may appear in this brief paper that I have ignored the planner and it is true that I refer to him explicitly only once. This is partly because I regard the so-called physical planner as a man apart only in so far as he finally organizes the hardware. The planner and the planning processes are however part of a conceptual wholeness which includes us all. In practice the shell and the kernel are necessarily and totally linked. To take an example from Kuwait, we find at the moment the demoliton of old buildings and the building of new, as a part of a replanning process. This involves the purchase of property for demolition and replacement. This is in a sense part of the physical planning process but it is also the main way in which State Revenue, derived almost entirely from oil, is released into the private sector and this has important economic consequences. Revenue is released into the private sector selectively because the channels are controlled by the nature of previous land ownership and this in turn has socio-logical consequences. Even if the planner is just to be thought of as a builder then the effects of what he does in fact spread far beyond the physical structures in quite obvious and simple ways. It is because of facts such as these that it becomes impossible to divorce physical planning from other aspects of planning either in urban studies or in any other.

Coming from the field of economic development, with experience mainly in the Middle East and Southern Asia, I have been progressively dissatisfied with two widely held beliefs concerning the towns of these regions. The first, which is widely held, is that the town is the centre of innovation and change and is therefore in the van of development. The second belief with which I have found myself dissatisfied is largely derived from the first, to wit that towns in developing countries become 'Westernized' or evolve from a 'pre-industrial' to an 'industrial' stage.

I believe that the root of the popularity of these, to my mind erroneous, generalizations lies in the compartmentalization of urban studies by the conventional disciplines subsumed under 'social sciences'. Each self-isolated approach tends to look for its own universalist truths and since until very recently each one of them has originated in the developed world, each has tended to seek and then to find those phenomena familiar to its own experience; what each discipline does in fact is to find what it is looking for usually in terms of economically advanced society. As an example, it might be held, without being hypercritical, that Sjoberg, [1] who made a considerable contribution with his development of the sociological concepts of 'Pre-Industrial City' and 'Industrial City', might have made it even greater if he had (and, in all, the evidence from the references shows he did not) consulted the considerable number of economic, geographical or planning studies of the city.

From the general intellectual point of view there may not be any need for haste in correcting the position; but if some of our assumptions concerning the nature of towns are invalid then any delay in correcting them will be very dangerous indeed to planned urbanization in the developing countries.

May I start by using as a convenient handle the following quotations from P. H. Mann's *An Approach to Urban Sociology*: [2]

'At the basic level of interaction, the economic values are the prime determinents of social value.'

'Seen from the viewpoint of economic achievement by any legal means the urban ethos would then favour an emphasis upon individualism....'

'The urban ethos, then, must be attuned to movement and change, and must be ready to accept this as a socially acceptable thing.'

'If it is accepted that social life based upon an appraisal of change requires a particular type of outlook, then the words of Wirth – tolerant, competitive, self-aggrandizing and exploitive – would seem more appropriate to urban than rural communities.'

Mann uses Sonakin's and Zimmerman's criteria of differences between rural and urban society in which occupational differences are stressed and he therefore accepts the town as an entity 'engaged principally in manufacturing, mechanical pursuits, and trade, commerce, professions and other non-agricultural occupations.'

While this is not an order of importance which all of us would want to accept, as a whole these occupations have become generally associated with advanced urbanism, and in particular with Sjoberg's 'industrial city'. When, therefore, so runs the argument, we find industrial city occupations, so too we find individualism, competition, innovation and acceptance of change, and an embarkation upon economic development of the only sort we know, in other words what some people would call 'Westernization'.

We are not concerned here with the economic development questions concerning sectoral labour surpluses or sectoral needs or intra-migration; we merely have to accept that in 'Western' economic experience – and here I would include that of the USSR, – economic development is associated with specialization, industrialization, commerce and urbanism. The developed world becomes associated with the 'industrial city', the underdeveloped or developing world with the 'pre-industrial' city.

Each discipline in turn has used those analytical techniques peculiar to itself in order to establish criteria, sometimes quantitative, sometimes not, which may then be employed in defining urbanism. The fascinating fact is this, that in whatever discipline is involved, function as indicated by occupational structure is a key factor. If one starts with Gordon Childe's [3] 'the mark of the city is its purposive social complexity' one arrives with Sjoberg [1] and Emrys Jones [4] in associating social class, mobility and distribution with occupations. If on the other hand one starts with the urban ecologists' distribution patterns of the classic type associated with Berry, Burgess, Hoyt or Smailes then these patterns appear not only as characterizing a structure within Wirth's 'social heterogeneity' but also as characterizing functions and occupation structures. All the arguments can be said to revolve around Mann's premise (a) which postulates an *economic* mainspring in urban life; to repeat : 'At the basic level of interaction, the economic values are the prime determinants of the social values' – and, one might add, of everything else.

Difficulties arise however when we turn to Mann's premiss (b) and when we start accepting a critical distinction in activities, attitudes and behaviour as between 'pre-industrial' and 'industrial' cities. Some of these difficulties arise from the formulation of over facile universalist concepts. McGee [5] has pointed out how in South-East Asia the impact of colonialism, in the form of the 'grafted city' or the 'implant city' for example, has made 'cities grow' despite their failure to industrialize, not because of industrialization, as they did in the Western countries'.

Accepting for the moment some exaggeration in this statement, it is nevertheless clear that behind the contrast lies a complex of historical and geographical factors which produce fundamental regional variations between, the West and Asia, South America and Asia.

In these latter areas certain gross distinctions between their forms of urbanism and that of the 'West' are clear enough even although the precise quantification of the difference between urbanism and pseudo-urbanization is extraordinarily difficult. In pseudo-urbanized communities one finds for example heavy disguised under-employment or unemployment – a phenomenon which however easily recognized is incredibly elusive for measurement – and this is particularly marked in the tertiary sector. The size of the tertiary sector, as measured by occupation, in pseudo-urbanized communities is usually very large – usually over 60 per cent, but this is no larger than in most Western urban centres. In pseudo-urban conditions one frequently finds that the rank – size rule cannot be applied and that it tends to be replaced by a primate city organization or ranking. One could extend the list of pseudo-urban characteristics very much further and associate them with regional differentiation.

My main purpose is however not to consider this but rather, in the context of the Middle East and Southern Asia, to challenge the association of 'individualism' and 'acceptance of change' with an urbanism which on the face of it has an economic mainspring, in fact to challenge the validity in this context of Alexander's 'Basic – Non-basic' concept. [6]

In South-West Asia we find not only the oldest urban centres in the world but also ancient towns and cities which have apparently transformed themselves or are transforming themselves, as far as morphology, function and occupational structure are concerned, for example Beirut, Cairo, Mashad, Damascus and Bombay, transforming themselves, that is, fairly slowly from a 'pre-Industrial' to an 'Industrial' level. On the other hand one can find towns and cities which have been whisked suddenly from obscurity to apparent full urbanism within a few decades, for example Ankara, Kuwait, Amman, Karachi and Tatangar; and lastly we have towns and cities in which rapid urbanization or even new creation is now taking place as with Ashdod, Abu Dhabi and Islamabad.

My belief is that we are witnessing not a sequence of 'a translation, a progression towards the patterns characteristic of the West', we are not seeing the appearance of the urban ethos described by Mann but are observing the birth of a new hybrid urbanism in which socio-economic values are, inter alia, *not* conducive to rapid economic development of the only kind we understand.

What of the relationship between socio-economic structure of the

EC H

town and economic development potential?

Even in the simplest communities there is and has been for millennia, in Margaret Mead's epigrammatic distinction, 'money in the community' though not a 'money-economy'. [7] The primeval rural peasant community, still numerically predominant in the part of the world under consideration is, in economic terms subsistence orientated, in sociological terms survival orientated. Minor specializations invariably exist, in primary production, in craft-industry secondary activities, and in commerce in the tertiary sector, but these are what are often called 'accidental' or 'incidental' specializations and purely economic contractual relationships hardly ever exist unless one is prepared to classify chattel slavery under this heading. Indissolubly linked with this economic organization is a social organisation based on primary contacts and with what I shall call at the moment a kinship/lineage/caste system. In the region with which I am concerned I think Sjoberg is wholly right in noting the importance of the extended family which, 'particularly that embraced by a single household, is an effective security agency'. One can go further however in dealing with the Middle East (including North Africa) and Southern Asia, and claim that the '*extended* extended-family'–the group which insists, by reference to actual or mythological lineage links, to common language or dialect or creed, on its separate identity. In this form this larger group as well as the smaller non-classificatory family is a standard socio-economic phenomenon in peasant societies without which survival even of the individual is very hazardous and forms a system which itself has a very strong survival value. This situation is basically non-urban.

When we turn to even simple money economies past and present in our region, we find a slightly more complex economic structure. Given material resources other than cultivable land then one finds market-oriented specialization. There will exist a significantly sized secondary, industrial sector and also a tertiary sector, represented at least by commerce, of some significant size and sophistication. There is therefore also implicit some degree of spatial concentration of activity and we then have the town–not the cult or garrison or administrative centre but the town. In the social structure of this simple urban unit, however, we can still observe the kinship/lineage/caste structure–which for reasons of brevity but also with some semantic significance I shall refer to henceforth as the caste structure –still playing a dominant role. In economic terms its function remains the same, the ensuring of the survival of the self-identified group, but now its organization widens so that caste becomes associated more and more with occupation on a 'closed-shop' principle.

Economic contractual relationships within the group remain very ill-developed but as between caste groups purely contractual relationships can thrive. In sociological terms primary contacts remain dominant within each group but as between groups secondary contacts either replace the primary – as Wirth would maintain – or, as I believe, are added to the primary. Morphologically, the association of caste and occupation then produces a complexity of distribution patterns within the town while spatially a new network of town-region relationships and networks appears.

Most of what I have described, and for which there is ample observational evidence, has been regarded as characteristic of what is very often called the 'pre-industrial' town. On the other hand we also know that much of it is also characteristic of 'Industrial' or 'Western' cities. The only considerable distinction lies in the apparent dominance within the Western city, first, in the economic field, of contractual relationships and, secondly, in the sociological field, of individualism and what has been called class consciousness as opposed to what I would call caste consciousness. In the non-Western city you have it reversed.

While this is a considerable distinction and while various specialists support the general thesis, the antithesis remains essentially a descriptive rather than an explanatory statement and it is very difficult to quantify and very difficult to apply.

First, quantification and application. To start once more with Sjoberg:

'The mobility and rapid change in the industrial world, combined
with the notion of universalism – i.e. judging each man
according to his training and ability – often runs counter to the
bonds of kinship.'

All depends now on what we mean by the industrial world. If the industrial world – here the town – is mainly concerned with tertiary activities rather than with esoteric technological industries, and if commercial, financial and administrative expertize is regarded as largely acquired by experience rather than by training then the bonds of kinship need not be bent let alone broken because kinship circles are still regarded even in parts of the industrial, Western world as excellent places for the acquirement of experience. Strong bonds of kinship, however, we intellectually associate with survival orientated socio-economies which are suspicious of innovation and antipathetic to change.

We know that the tertiary sector is a great and growing part of advanced economies. A *Commentary on Occupation by Industrial Matrices* by the Manpower Research Unit has pointed out that, in Britain,

Group 1 Occupation [Proprietors, Managers and Executive Staff], for which there is only very slight vocational training, take up 11 per cent of the labour force and have a growth rate of 1·5 per cent per annum. Group 2 [Clerical and allied occupations], again for which training is not of any highly specialized kind, takes up 15 per cent of the labour force and has a growth rate of *c.* 2 per cent. Group 3 [Professional and higher technical occupations] is the only one of the seven groups in which reasonably high order training and ability of any relevance to Sjoberg's theory is of vital significance. This group has a growth rate of *c.* 3·5 per cent per annum, but only includes 5 per cent of the labour force.

Utilizing a different approach Carter [8] has found that only about 9 per cent of Welsh towns may be regarded as centres of technologically advanced industry; almost all the others are dominated by tertiary activity. The data, such as it is, of analysis of occupations by sector generally seems to suggest that training and ability in a Sjoberg sense is not necessarily in much greater demand in urbanized developed societies than it is in the developing countries.

Commonsense, on the other hand, tells us that this is an absurd conclusion. In anti-change under-developed societies, there is we know, a shortage of skill on the one hand and a brain-drain on the other, both necessarily associated with the urban centres. Equally, we know that urban employment in the change-accepting developed countries is associated more and more with training and career individualism and less and less with family background experience. But, there is at the moment, even in statistically well-served countries, no data other than that obtainable from un-coordinated small scale surveys which throws any quantitative light on economic and social behaviour linked with economic and social function. Any sort of accurate quantification is of course absolutely impossible for the developing countries. We are thereafter left with Moser and Wolf Scott [9] who stress the blurring that appears when social and economic differences between British towns are statistically studied, with Mann who finds that the relative importance of agriculture is the only absolutely clear indicator of difference between conurbations and regions, and with Wibberley, who probably makes the most significant comment of all:

'In highly developed countries a common culture is arising between town and countryside – a culture that is neither urban nor rural.' [10]

It may be that in some developed countries a homogeneity of this kind may be growing alongside the urban heterogeneity that Wirth finds. What is certain is that the sort of quantification of the socio-economic characteristics of the 'Western' city which might indicate critical thresholds in attitudes to and potential for economic growth is at the moment impossible.

In the Middle East and other developing regions one is then left only with a certain number of indicators of socio-economic behaviour, indicators which suggest that Sjoberg, Mann, Hanson, McGee and many others have, *in toto* but not separately, arrived somewhere near the broad truth that pseudo-urbanization can statistically appear very similar to what we term Western urbanization, that the strength of non-contractual relationships is the special mark of some towns and cities, that this strength derives from social insecurity and lack of economic opportunity, and that such insecurity and lack of opportunity are not symptomatic of a low evolutionary level but are rooted in what I shall call geographical fact and are moreover factors tending to stultify economic growth and development.

First, briefly, what are the indicators? There is in the first place a group which can be termed morphological or distributional. Beirut is an ancient city with an occupational structure which, as far as can be ascertained from poor data, approximates to that of London. Its tertiary sector is well-developed and, statistically speaking, well-stocked with expertise. However, as Mrs Hurst [11] has pointed out, the spatial distribution of 'income shows no significant correlation with family size, estivage, mobility, previous address, house ownership or building age'. Add to this, observations by Mrs Hurst and Chehab-ed-Dine [12] that the Centre is occupied by high income groups and the periphery by low and middle income families, a complete antithesis to the model Western city. Within Beirut there exist fourteen officially recognized distinct communities, mainly religion and therefore kinship based, as well as many others; what I have called a caste element is recognizable in the way in which these communities, most of them of very ancient standing, are associated with occupational and city quarter groupings. This in a city where terms such as savings, investment, and profit, have exactly the same apparent semantic significance as they have in Wall Street or the City of London. Here we can find in fact some spatial, morphological indicators of non-Western urbanism.

Secondly, there is a group of indicators which are both morphological and socio-economic, a group which may be exemplified by the souk or bazaar unit. In Karachi, occupationally more heavily engaged in manufacturing than many Western cities, the physical growth of the city, particularly during the period when it served as capital, included some elements of what sociologists would term 'class' rather than 'caste' separation, in particular exemplified by a peripheral quarter with embassies and high-income residential housing. But here, as also may be found in Jordanian Amman, there is an invasion by traditional elements. The spearhead is formed by neighbourhood or daily-requirement retail shops in the main catering for menials and this is then followed by the growth of miniature souks whose characteristic is that in them are combined low-income residence, workshops and retail outlets and which are associated with 'caste' occupation groups. These complexes move into the new 'class' differentiated zones and as they grow reduce the early distinctiveness of the new suburbs.

Thirdly, there are the indicators which are socio-economic and behavioural, illustrated in this case from Kuwait. In this essentially new city there have been implemented a very large number of physical planning measures which are producing a city which is beginning superficially to look like a 'Western' city. In main occupational structure the primary, secondary, tertiary breakdown is again very comformable with 'Western' patterns. The most significant economic fact that emerges from an analysis of the 1965 employment census is that with five exceptions all types of establishment are very small, averaging only 4·2 employees per establishment. As in Egypt, industrial establishments are predominantly family affairs, the exceptions being, the manufacturing of beverages and of cement – asbestos pipes, oil refining, commercial banking and fish-food processing (here associated with the single Kuwait Gulf shrimp factory). None of these activities with the exception of oil refining can be regarded as a breeding-ground for any economic elite or 'take-off' group. While this is not necessarily important to Kuwait such a situation can create great problems for less well-endowed countries; as Dhar and Lydall [13] have pointed out, any secondary sector which is dominated by the small factory is utilising the industries which 'use more capital *and* more labour per unit of output than large factories'. In Kuwait detailed analysis shows that even in manufacturing groups such as manufacturing of metals, machinery, etc., that these are essentially repair trades rather than production centres.

If one then sets this economic data in the context of other population characteristics then I would suggest a further correlation may be observed. In 1965, 52·9 per cent of the population of Kuwait was non-Kuwaiti in citizenship. Of these 31·4 per cent were Jordanians, mainly insecure political refugees from Palestine, 12·5 per cent Iranians, mainly poor immigrants from harsh southern Iran, 9·5 per cent Indians and Pakistanis, endogenously inclined and family structured immigrants whatever varied skills they may have had. Here one has the epitome of the insecurity and lack of opportunity which I earlier postulated. In Kuwait it led to the manning of the radio service exclusively by Iraqis and the television service exclusively by Egyptians, this on a closed shop basis even to each other, the whole pattern being reminiscent of the Egyptian guilds which survived into the twentieth century and of the present-day exclusive merchant family groups so characteristic of South-West Asia.

These are only illustrations of a situation which is becoming amply documented but they serve to lead up to my main hypothesis. In the Middle East, millennia of experience and complex commerce and finance has produced a special brand of urbanism which is not the 'colonial transplant' of McGee, neither is it 'Western' urbanism, nor is it simply 'pre-industrial'. It has been characterized by a socio-economic ability continuously to adapt and adjust a survival-orientated, non-contractual economy and society so that in the tertiary and to some extent in the secondary economic sectors apparent sophistication is attained but non-contractual links are not destroyed. On the whole I find that this non-fundamental adaptation is still being made even although it is being challenged by 'Westernization' through State planning policies. We know that in the case of peasant societies non-contractual socio-economic structures are generally hostile to innovation. What of the cities of under-developed countries? Figuratively speaking, one can here think of quasi-urbanism as having acquired through a series of minor changes, live virus infections, a high resistance to serious infection by major change – acquiring resistance to change. Both on the micro and macro scale such a diagnosis can explain many of the strange phenomena observable in the under-developed or developing world. The case of Japan may then be regarded as exceptional in that the 'family' social structure has become sufficiently changed to allow for innovation, this is mainly because the economic unit, the firm, has taken over many of the sociological attributes of the family without losing its economic strength. In the middle East this has not happened.

If this hypothesis is at all valid then it has serious implications for economic development policies. It may well be that in some regions urban centres are not the loci where innovation or change will take place but rather may be the strongholds of obstruction to innovation and change. It may also be true that innovation and individualism can only be expected to grow where some very special types of secondary sector activity, of manufacturing industry, make a demand for very highly specialized expertise of a career type. This cannot easily happen everywhere and can only quickly happen where there are considerable advantages provided by resource and by location.

At this point I must refuse to explore the paths of regional resource differentiation which open out before us even though I believe them to be vitally important. Our concern must remain with my main hypothesis and the moral which I wish to draw.

The attitudes and values to which Mrs Glass and Dr Ceccarelli have referred and which are the essential elements in an understanding of urbanization appear in many different forms. They sometimes appear in direct actions which are sometimes difficult to measure but always they are manifest in structures which are recognizable, for example family or class stratification, or in urban morphology, organization and all other planes including political, economic and cultural activities. If we, as social scientists, could in cooperation feed in the input data from different disciplines then we might not only be able to quantifiably prove or disprove my hypothesis, something which is impossible at the moment, but further than that, it could clear the ground quite considerably. One of the most profound remarks made by Professor Arberry was his comment that in Arab folk tales there is no question of reward following merit but only of heaven-sent fortune or disaster – essentially a passive concept. If we could put our heads together and work out a common measure of our value systems then it might be possible to find how much of this sort of attitude is deep, basic and cultural and unlikely to be changed or how much is superficial and easily changed by planned changes in environment.

When this happens then we can understand and plan a Middle East town. Until such time one is always in fact going to be planning as an alien and pretending to an understanding which we do not possess.

REFERENCES

1. G. Sjoberg, *The Pre-Industrial City*. The Free Press of Glencoe, Illinois.
2. P.H. Mann, *An Approach to Urban Sociology* (London, 1965).
3. V. Gordon Childe, 'The Urban Revolution', *Town Planning Review*, (1950).
4. Emrys Jones, *Towns and Cities*, O.U.P., 1966.
5. T.G. McGee, *The South-East Asian City* (London, 1967).
6. J.W. Alexander, 'The Basic-Nonbasic Concept of Urban Economic Functions', *Econ. Geog.*, xxx (1954).
7. Margaret Mead, *Cultural Patterns and Technical Change*, UNESCO, 1955.
8. H. Carter, *The Towns of Wales*, Univ. of Wales Press, 1965.
9. C.A. Moser and W. Scott, 'British Towns, a Statistical Study of their Social and Economic Differences' (London, 1961).
10. G.P. Wibberley, 'Change in the structure and Functions of the Rural Community', *Sociologia Ruralis*, 11, 2 (1960).

11. E. W. Eliot Hurst, '*The Urban Geography of Beirut*, M.Litt. Thesis, Univ. of Durham, 1966.

12. Said Chehab-ed-Dine, *Géographie Humaine de Beyrouth* (Beirut, 1960).

13. P. N. Dhar and H. F. Lydall, *The Role of Small Enterprises in Indian Economic Development* (London, 1961).

Village, Town or Settlement Systems?

DAVID THORPE

Settlements in the modern world are changing so rapidly that our conception of their real character will frequently run in advance of the terms which are available to categorize their differences. This is particularly true of urban settlements, and partly because of the devouring spatial spread of urban orientated activity is true of all settlement. A problem of this kind was recognized in the nineteenth century and before. For example, the Registrar General [1] in the 1851 Census of Population report distinguished, on the one hand, a clear cut traditional hierarchy of village, market town, country town and metropolis and, on the other hand, an uncertain rapidly growing group of new 'populous districts' of an 'adventitious character'. Today, as more powerful statistical techniques become available, this problem has a growing importance. Many of the characteristics such techniques enable us to establish will very heavily depend on the boundary decisions made by the investigator. The availability of data by grid reference, rather than administrative units, will not necessarily ease the situation, for boundary decisions will still have to be made. To a considerable degree the problem is that into which we are forced by the existence of vague terms either, in everyday speech, like hamlet, village, town, city and suburb or in slightly more restricted use, like conurbation, urban region and city region. Indeed there are almost as many definitions of some of these terms at textbook level as textbooks. [2]

There is clearly no easy solution to this problem although it is far less of a problem once it is appreciated. A solution once offered was that of an 'urban-rural continuum' [3] with settlements placed relative to that continuum. This, however, does not offer much operational support to the research worker for it fails to recognize that economic and social discontinuities may be of great importance *within* settlements. Pahl has demonstrated this in respect of the social features of settlements in the Outer London region. [4]

A number of investigations have suggested solutions to the problem by stressing the non-spatial characteristics of different settlement types. Thus Dyos, [5] noting that to identify the suburb on the ground is not easy, supports a suggestion that 'suburban may be defined as a state of existence' but even he adds 'within a few minutes' walk of the railway station, the shops and the fields'. Pahl[6] favours the examination of the 'state of mind' of the members of different groups existing in a settlement, and stresses the need for the temporal examination of village activities – 'if there is a continuum then it is more likely to have a temporal rather than a spatial basis'. Webber writes of 'the urban place and the *nonplace urban realm*'. He suggests that most recent social and technological changes are in fact neutral in their spatial impacts and that the essential qualities of urbanness are cultural in character, not technical and that these qualities are not necessarily tied to the conceptions that see the city as a spatial phenomenon.

These suggestions, useful for their own purposes, do not seem to be totally satisfactory for attempts to provide syntheses of settlement characteristics. [8] Such attempts probably must be based on 'place'. This, in fact, is not too great a distortion for:

(*a*) place need not be defined in real distance terms but can easily incorporate time / distance and cost / distance measurements. (It will however be more difficult to incorporate psychological distance – a concept of equal importance.) Thus, although cities may not follow real distance nodal concentric forms (Webber), cities or urban-regions will be structured in time or cost / distance terms.

(*b*) although attitudes of mind are very important they are probably spatially located and spatially sorted by land values, mutual repulsion or attraction, or by local (e.g. government) policies. Thus Pahl's concept that '*meaningful* location of communities is changing so that the attitude to the crossing of space is changing within the different social groups' [9] poses a locational problem, of importance, albeit through a social filter.

(*c*) many of our conceptual problems arise from clinging to a Euclidean space with rigid shapes (e.g. the typical topographical map). A great many workers [10] are now forging techniques by which data can be presented and analysed without such restrictions (e.g. at a simple level the 'map transformation' of the population cartogram for the presentation of election results). The techniques are important but even more important is the conceptual freedom they allow and foster.

The approach to settlement analysis which is to be suggested below is then founded on these problems. Specifically it depends on the following propositions:

(*a*) a great proportion of human activity is spatially bound (e.g. that 'distance' is an important control sometimes of the level of demand and sometimes of the form of organization adopted by suppliers).

(*b*) that this leads to the establishment of settlement features which we recognize at a highly subjective level.

(*c*) that although each separate activity may have distinctive characteristics the great majority of activities do combine into a few meaningful broad systems.

(*d*) that human activities exist in *spatially over*-lapping systems and that elements in the settlements which appear on the ground are variously attributable to different broad systems.

(*e*) that broad activity systems can be recognized and isolated as important formative agents for different settlement systems.

From the definition of my problem, and this statement of the foundations of my approach to a solution, it is important to distinguish as quickly as possible my main settlement systems. Each requires a more lengthy presentation than is possible here. The systems are of two orders. The first places emphasis on *between* settlement space and the second on *within* settlement space. [11] This distinction is to some extent artificial but is sufficiently real for it to enable us to focus attention on many of the processes which result in systems of different kinds. The systems can be listed:

Table 1

A. Between settlement space	B. Within settlement space
1. Rural	5. Town or city region
2. Encampment	6. Urbanized region
3. Urban	
4. Industrial Zone	

The focus in the case of the first type of system (i.e. that characterized by a view of between settlement space) is on nodules of settlement as complete units. The character of these units is determined by the relative importance and forms of interconnections which occur between them. Thus there exist in the rural settlement system a succession of nodules from farm to country town which are all in a significant mutual relationship.

The focus in the second type of system (i.e. that characterized by a view of within settlement space) is in a sense on a finer scale. Here, the character of the system results from the relationships which exist between the various parts of areas of what are essentially single settlements. When complex urban settlements were small in spatial extent this type of settlement could certainly involve a finer meshed study. As urban regions grow to cover large areas of territory the scale of effective study will frequently have to be more general than before. This change in scale will have great consequences for the type of information research workers can provide society about its settlements.

A. BETWEEN SETTLEMENT SPACE

1. *The Rural Settlement System.* Historically most activity and settlement was based on an agricultural economy. This led to a highly characteristic pattern (although its precise form might vary locally considerably). The pattern was characterized by dispersal with considerable 'distances' between the settlement nuclei. These nuclei might include isolated farmsteads, hamlets, villages, market towns and county towns. As members of this system, the market and county towns only existed to serve it. Any other functions they might have added do not fall in this category conceptually and thus lie outside the system. An understanding of such functions can only be firmly based when they are placed in their own particular operational system (one which presumably will usually be an urban-industrial one). Today this system, is of course, in decline in Western economies. The decline arises from increases in labour productivity and a consequent smaller labour force employed in agriculture, which, via local multipliers, leads to a relative fall in service employment. It is also in decline because of the changing nature of 'distance' within the system. Some steps in the system are no longer necessary because of concentration in production (e.g. larger farms) and of changing marketing techniques (e.g. contractual selling). This has frequently meant the by-passing of smaller market towns. Indeed in many cases the county towns themselves have experienced a similar fate and specialist marketing establishments have been set up at a level above the county town. My point is, in summary, that our conception of the countryside as an area of settlement has not yet caught up with the dramatic decline in the farm labour force.

2. *Encampment Settlement Systems.* The plural here is deliberate for a number of different activity groups give rise to settlements which have many similarities. The settlement pattern is one characterized by smallish, isolated usually markedly homogeneous, units which do not fulfil significant functions for a surrounding territory. In the last characteristic they are therefore distinct from the market town. The activities may include mining, defence, handcraft industry and recreation of a not highly commercial nature. They all are site rather than situation orientated. For conceptual purposes it is important to distinguish encampment settlements which, although linked into wider systems, are for some activities especially inward looking.

They are thus particularly clearly superimposed on, rather than integrated with, other settlements. When situation is important, encampments become conceptually part of a wider system than this (e.g. the mining village economically will be part of an industrial zone but socially may be an encampment.) The mining village, and here the popular name is very significant even for 'towns' like Ashington (population 27,000), as an encampment settlement is characterized by extreme homogeneity, by traditionally very short journey to work movement and by a high degree of local service self-sufficiency. As the journey to work pattern is changed by pit closures some change does occur but it is very limited, for the journey is frequently a sealed movement in a special National Coal Board coach. More important fundamental changes occur as a result of the introduction of elements of other settlement systems into declining coalfield areas and by the slow adjustment of mining encampment forms to forms more easily adaptable to those other systems.

Military encampments are important settlement features in their own right, frequently with an internal pattern and dynamic very different to any other form. They are also part of a system which will include isolated but related units and married quarters etc. This is a system which has spatial characteristics which are very similar to many other systems but which is based on the site requirements (at least in peacetime) of the main camp.

The growing importance of recreation (including 'retirement') as a settlement foundation is again site orientated and will frequently also be related only obliquely to other forms of settlement in an area. All forms of encampment settlement appear to have an interesting characteristic of being relatively transitory features.

3. *The Urban Settlement System.* This is characteristic by being independent from the rural system, by having nuclei which are larger than the encampment (by how much?) and by being economically and socially far more heterogeneous than the encampment. An alternative name for it, which I have discarded as being too contradictory, was that of 'the Independent Town System'. Clearly no town is independent in an absolute sense. Some, however, can perhaps be distinguished as having important characteristics which are relatively independent from immediate surrounds. Probably the earliest examples of the activity involved here can be seen in centres of 'conspicuous consumption' related to a court or major religious house. Slightly later the merchantile town represents an important example. More normally today we can only think of independent sectors of urban economies. Thus here are those which evolved from industries which initially only a local (rural servicing) market, and

which now serve national or international markets. Such industries, 'old established' or 'native', [12] are typically agricultural engineering or food manufacturing. They are often represented by the large plants which dominate the industrial structure of towns isolated from industrial zones. Other industries which fall into this category are 'modern native' and have appeared usually without careful location decision taking. In their case the stimulus for foundation is found in a wide range of personal factors. For both types it is not easy to distinguish local and 'independent' components without far more input – output data at plant level than is presently available. Consider a town like Carlisle in which local servicing is important but which also has a relatively important independent manufacturing sector.

What proportion of its 13,000 employees in manufacturing are in reality independent from its regional role?

Table 2

	Industrial group	Insured employees
VI	Engineering	1,226
VII	Vehicles	1,191
VIII	Other metal goods	1,555
X	Textiles	2,674
XII	Clothing	600
XIII	Food, drink, tobacco	4,036
III–XVI	Manufacturing	12,921
VII–XXIV	Services, trades and professions	22,417

This is an easy question to pose. Some plants will serve only local markets, others will serve national or international markets, and some will service intermediate markets. To demonstrate this by an input – output matrix with suitable regional boundaries is however likely to be very difficult for each plant and activity. Such difficulties however, should not prevent us from realising the reality of this type of settlement.

Independent is unfortunately a word which has considerable emotional overtones, although some of these will we hope be removed by a more firmly based local government structure, we ought therefore to be more careful in its use. What is the meaningful distance from urban regions at which *independent* becomes a useful description of spatial activity? What do we really mean by terming a new town independent from an existing one?

4. *The Industrial Zone System.* During the nineteenth century many

settlement complexes developed as closely linked industrial zones but within which the various nodules of settlement existed largely isolated for everyday social contacts. The industrial linkage involved inter plant flows of products and services. It was not a simple spatial coexistence of industries because of common requirements (the line of division here is however slight). We are very familiar with this situation historically in the locational specialization of different areas of the Lancashire Cotton Industrial Zone, or of the admixture of activity typical of the Yorkshire Woollen Industrial Zone, or the close connections within the coalfields of pit and port via waggonway or railway. Such historical spatial connections frequently found expression in the activities of 'captains of industry'. A family like the Pease's of Darlington could thus own coalmines (in S. W. Durham), promote a railway (Stockton-Darlington) build a port-town (Middlesbrough) and sponsor a holiday resort development (Saltburn).

Today important changes in industry have altered this structure to a considerable degree. The increasing size of plant tends to make each plant more locally independent (connections are within plants or firms rather than between plants or firms). Working slightly against these processes of independence are those which have resulted in more industrial activities involving the assembly of sub-components and more products involving multiple materials (e.g.

Table 3. Per cent tonnage from or to the region

Category	Input materials		Output goods	
	Manufactured	All	Intermediate	All
Food	21	71	23	29
Tobacco	39	71		
Chemicals	42	73	1	15
Metal	0	100	5	
Paper	89	84	49	
Paper products	45	45	22	
Other industries	25	43	14	12
Mechanical engineering	11		12	
Electrical engineering	18		13	
Textiles	0		0	
Clothing	17		0	17
Footwear	25		65	17
Furniture	12		0	2

to everything a packet!). Both changes however unite to considerably widen the area of close linkage. Thus Britton [13] for the Bristol
region (Somerset and Gloucestershire) has published linkage data
as set out in Table 3.

Data which must lead us to the conclusion that with one or two
exceptions the significant linkage pattern is over a far wider area
than just the local region. Similarly the Teesside Survey found that
within Teesside only 9 per cent of Heavy Industry employment was
attributable to local linkage and 4 per cent for other industry. [14]
One interesting suggestive delimitation of wider industrial zones is
that of Lultrell's analysis [15] of branch factories in the early 1950s:

Table 4. Distance in miles of branches from parent factories by
organizational type

	Under 30	30–74	75–149	150 and over	Total
Subsidiary	14	9	3	2	28
Intermediate semi-independent	5	7	3	8	23
Self-contained (duplication of product or separate range)	2	4	5	19	30

Industrial zones appeared then in terms of the organisational
pattern of the branch factory. The widely heralded advantages of
growth points are another reflection of the industrial zone process.
But how large are the *points*? Are they *points* on maps of 1:100,000,
1:1M, 1:10M, 1:100M or 1:1,000M?

Economically the extent of the modern industrial zone is therefore
something very much wider than that of the nineteenth century form.
The nineteenth-century industrial zone did however develop certain
special social features. These frequently linger on and may in fact
be appearing in the wider economic zones today as well. As vestiges
from the past they are frequently of great present important. They
involve an extra-ordinary balance of sub-area social independence
and inter-dependence. This balance arises largely from the high
population densities of the zones. American investigations of social
contacts over distance have emphasised how the density of population appears to be an important controlling feature of local social
interactions. Thus in such areas intervening opportunity models
appear more successful in representing reality than gravity models. [16] This indeed is what folk-law suggests. The strength of

EC I

local community identity in such 'towns' as Wallsend, Bolton, Halifax or Stockton was, and is, great. Frequently such areas support separate major shopping centres of some size, and numbers of their inhabitants probably have extremely insular movement patterns. This then is sub-area independence. The total identity arises because of the ease with which the public can recognize the existence of a Tyneside or Clydeside Industrial Zone as compared with a London region. The overall high densities are important here as contributing factors.

B. WITHIN SETTLEMENT SPACE

5. *The Town or City Region System*. This fifth settlement system is based on a slightly different focus – with settlement space. It is the simple case of a single node settlement in which activities are aligned in space relative to that node. The classic generalizations [17] of Burgess (concentric ring formation) and Hoyt (sectors) are therefore directly useful in the interpretation of the pattern. The pattern is one which may well be fairly extensive in space. It must include all commuter suburbs, and perhaps the weekend recreation zone (including in many societies the area of weekend cottages). It does so not because these are precisely the same as other town elements but because they can only fundamentally be understood as part of the town system (e.g. presumably if the desire to live in the country and work in the town is one held by a certain proportion of particular socio-economic groups then that desire in total should not vary too greatly from town to town with similar social groupings. Our focus on the whole system would however enable us to spotlight any variations which did exist and to demonstrate variations which exist between different types of town.)

The utility of the Burgess and Hoyt generalization is frequently questioned. [18] Sometimes their bases are misunderstood and they are seen to be incompatible. This is unfortunate because they do enable us to focus on different scales of the internal spatial structure of the town system (as indeed does the third generalization of Harris and Ullman's multiple nucleii. [19] The concentric processes of centrifugal and centripetal pulls do operate within towns at a general level. For some purposes of analysis it is sufficient simply to recognise them. Sectoring appears to result from the operation of less general more individual decisions. It will in particular lead to distortions in concentric patterns as such decisions are taken independently over time. These decisions may however be completely in alignment with the influence of the central node. Thus in the extension of built-in areas a particular sector may grow far more rapidly than others simply by fringe developments occuring randomly in relation to an existing fringe – there never being at any one time sufficient development to warrant complete annular growth. The decisions may of course be influenced by other factors as well, particularly linkages between spatially related activities. Such linkages do however generally appear to operate at a rather less general level than centrifugal / centripetal forces.

Harris and Ullman's generalization is rather different from the other two for it emphasizes the mutual attraction and repulsion of different functions. As such it is operating on a less generalized level. If, however, we consider only the attractions and repulsions between the central area and each other land use, rather than within the whole matrix of land uses as they suggest, there is a situation very similar to that of the other two schemes (the whole matrix does indeed seem to be more applicable at an urban region level of complexity than at the town level).

The town and the city region are two slightly different forms of what is basically the same system. Within a town land uses may be found to have some specific mutual relationship. Increasingly these relationships extend further than the limit of the continuously built-up area (the border of the town). This extension into a city region has important consequences for the overall settlement pattern. Basically integral elements of the town are often found at a considerable distance from it. These elements will lie spatially in some recognizable pattern. This pattern could be used to define the new extent to the town. Many have recently sought to define city regions in such a way for administrative purposes. They have used, as a basic premise, the fact that the town and the country are now far more mutually linked than ever before. This is clear, but what is equally clear is that the city region is not a settlement of the old type with definable boundaries and a simple physical identity. It is a system and as such overlaps with other systems which although linked to it may often be antagonistic to it. [20] The rural system, for instance, is frequently in conflict with the urban.

6. *The Urbanized Region System*. The town system is largely understandable in terms of relationships with the central node and for this reason presents a relatively easily examinable case. The urbanized region is fundamentally different (although two separate town systems as they interlock may begin to approach it in form). In its case a high level multi-nodal structure exists. Connections can only be appreciated in intensity terms rather than absolutes. Different activities within the system exist immediately unrelated in space in the same territory. Complex inter-area movements are established and individuals lead spatially fragmented lives. Each activity and the de-

mand for it will have a spatial dimension but these will to a considerable extent be separate from other activities (i.e. no single
absolutely dominant node). There is therefore a considerable loosening of the overall settlement structure but at largely unknown, and
rapidly changing, social and economic activity cost patterns. Such
problems are most apparent in the service industries, including
in particular the distributive trades and local administration and
government.

As yet the description and analysis of urbanized region patterns
of this sort is poorly advanced. A generalization such as Harris
and Ullman's does offer some pointers to a possible approach. Mutual
antagonism and attraction are clearly important to the urban region
scale. Probably however we will have to make people far more aware
of the very varying forms and shapes that urban regions can take
before basic analysis advances much further. Thus there are the seven
plan alternatives of the Washington Year 2000 Plan [21]:

   1 Restricted growth
   2 New independent (sic.) cities
   3 Planned sprawl
   4 Dispersed cities
   5 Ring of cities
   6 Peripheral communities
   7 Radial corridor plan

Or there are Kevin Lynch's [22] six possible structures:

   1 Dispersed sheet
   2 Galaxy
   3 Core city
   4 Urban star
   5 The ring
   6 The multi-centred unit

Clearly each of these offers certain advantages and disadvantages,
while each may be more or less useful in a given situation. Dangers
are apparent in accepting uncritically one or two 'normal' forms.
Far more important would seem to be local attempts to articulate the
particular form a given urban region takes, or indeed even to be
clear on the distinctions between urban regions and the traditional
concentric / sector town. Furthermore it should be realized that
many activities and entrepreneurs are already operating on some
particular form of urban region (and perhaps a specific form each)
in every area approaching that state. More growth (planned or un-
planned) will alter these operations but not necessarily absolutely
change them. Total coordination may well not be possible. More
important may well be a pattern which allows each activity to operate

as successfully as possible without causing hidden costs to other activities.

CONCLUSIONS

The six systems outlined above attempt to encompass conceptually most of the important spatial features of settlement forming activity. No single system can be expected to be found in a pure form in a given locality. Reality is always an admixture of such systems. Specifically in terms of urban growth all six systems are involved. Spatially such growth implies a growing juxtaposition of systems but not necessarily their disappearance. A considerable amount of research is necessary before the full significance of this can probably be appreciated. However, much that has been conducted may gain a wider significance from such an overview as this. The six systems can be conceived as filters of reality. Any given locality will be, via its various elements, attributable to a number of systems. Of particular importance here is the overlap between systems 5 and 6 (the town and urban region). As a town becomes more complex in structure it takes on more and more of the form of the urban region. The change is gradual but real, and because of its gradual nature very hard to distinguish. No terms are available to summarize it in such simple forms as the traditional hierarchy of village, market town, country town and metropolis. Those seeking solutions to problems like local government re-organization must fully appreciate the implications of this. A few standard settlement models are not sufficient to encompass present realities. One wonders therefore whether any standard solutions might be possible or whether it will be necessary to structure powers and areas of responsibility in many varying ways with each suitable for a particular locality.

Discussion of the problems of towns and regions is today so frequently handicapped by misconceptions, arising from terminology and jargon, that all who work in this field should consider carefully the real meaning that they wish to communicate. The present paper has attempted to provide one type of framework to assist in this task. The synthesis which it has attempted has involved the introduction of another jargon. This one hopes will be discarded but that the concepts and the framework will prove useful to the increasingly important task of communicating to society the realities of the places in which it lives.

REFERENCES

1. Registrar General, *Census of Great Britain 1851*, Population Tables
    Vol. 1, 1852, pp vlx–xlviii.
2. L. D. Stamp, *A Glossary of Geographical Terms*, 1961.
3. *United Nations Population Studies*, No. 8, 1950, p 2.
4. R. E. Pahl, 'The Rural-Urban Continuum', *Sociologia Ruralis*, vol. 6,
    1966, pp 299–327.
5. H. J. Dyos, *Victorian Suburb*, 1961, p 21.
6. P. M. Pahl, op. cit., p 304.
7. M. M. Webber, 'Urban Place and Nonplace Urban Realm' in
    Explorations into Urban Structure, ed. M. M. Webber, 1964,
    pp 79–153.
8. See also the discussions noted in H. J. Dyos (ed.), *The Study of Urban
    History*, 1968, for instance pp 278–9.
9. R. E. Pahl, 'Class and Community in English Commuter Villages',
    Sociologia Ruralis, Vol. v, 1965, p 6.
10. See P. Haggett, *Location Analysis in Human Geography*, 1965, and
    W. Bunge, *Theoretical Geography*, Lund Studies in Geography, Series
    C, and Mathematical Geography, 1. Occasional Paper, No. 8.
11. See David Thorpe, *The Geographer and Urban Studies*, Department of
    Geography, University of Durham, 1966, for an account of some
    of the implications of this division for urban geography.
12. H. D. Watts, 'The Character and Origin of Industry in a Rural
    Area – A case study of East Yorkshire', *Yorkshire Bulletin of
    Economic and Social Research*, Vol. 18, No. 2, Nov. 1966, p. 122.
13. J. N. H. Britton, *Regional Analysis and Economic Geography*, 1967.
14. I am indebted to Mr A. R. Townsend for these data.
15. W. F. Luttrell, *Factory Location and Industrial Movement*, Vol. 1, 1962.
    Note, however that his sample of firms was locationally biased in
    a number of ways.
16. See the review by G. Olsson, *Distance and Human Interaction*, Regional
    Science Research Institute, Bibliographical Series, No. 2, 1965.
17. E. W. Burgess, 'The Growth of the City' in R. E. Pack, E. W.
    Burgess and R. D. McKenzie, *The City*, 1925; and H. Hoyt,
    The Structure and Growth of Residential Neighbourhoods in American Cities
    1939.
18. These criticisms are usefully summarized in L. F. Schnore, 'On the
    Spatial Structure of Cities in the Two Americas', Chapter 10 of P. M.
    Hauser and L. F. Schnore (eds), in *The Study of Urbanisation*, 1965.
19. C. D. Harris and E. L. Ullman, 'The Nature of Cities', *Annals of
    American Academy of Political and Social Science*, 1945, Vol. 242,
    pp 7–17.
20. This sentence was added to the original paper to meet points
    raised by Mr Sharpe's paper.
21. Quoted in P. Hall, 'Planning for Urban Growth : Metropolitan
    Plans and Their Implications for South East England', *Regional
    Studies*, Vol. 1, No. 2, Dec. 1967, pp 101–34.
22. K. Lynch, 'The Pattern of the Metropolis' in *The Future Metropolis*
    (ed. L. Rodwin), 1962.

Discussion

C. N. SAUNDERS
I am faced all the time with the problem of planning decisions. One would like to think that today we were able to make a very much better decision than Professor Abercrombie was able to make in his day. I think the limited knowledge we have got, the data, the techniques, knowledge of social satisfactions and our knowledge of economic function has not progressed much since his time. This has happened during a period when of course the whole complex we are working in has evolved very considerably.

I would just mention one example – the problem of the third London airport. When this came along we wondered about the significance of the decision in regional planning terms. (I suppose that regional planning is the same as urban growth as far as the south of England is concerned.) The sad story of course is that very little has been recorded of the effects of Heathrow on the social, economic and the physical field in the south-east.

Dr Thorpe and Professor Bowen-Jones have been trying to throw light on categorization and structure of settlements of societies and how economies behave. This brings to mind the very real problems that face academic research in this field. Urban growth is really meaningless today; we are dealing with settlement growth. It is not just growth it is also 'change'. If you call it growth you tend to think of what is new but in any urban area you do not get growth alone – it is the change in the core which is the only way in which the growth of the peripheries or elsewhere can take place. For instance, is the development of Peterborough the growth of Peterborough or is it a London growth? On Dr Thorpe's point, as to whether one ought to make any distinction at all, it is just part of the national settlement growth and I think it is very difficult to try and separate because it makes the job of the academic researcher terribly difficult.

Two simple points I think I would like to isolate – firstly – we all recognize that we are dealing with a dynamic and not a static system. This is very much more easily said that in fact recognized. The second point I would make is not dissimilar. Do we truly grasp the importance of recognizing the organic nature of growth rather than the mechanistic approach implied in the concept of 'doughnuts' and 'stars'. The reality is that 'patterns' only exist in one point in time. It does not exist over a period.

This takes me back to the very first paper which we had from Dr Ceccarelli. I suspect that he was thinking of the professionals in this field looking at the growth settlement as an evolving system through time. The unenviable task I suppose of the social sciences is to have to create the necessary generation of ideas and studies throughout this whole field which will help the practising planners and politicians to make better decisions than they do at the moment.

J. T. COPPOCK

Looking at the impact of urban growth on rural land use, it is estimated that the rate of agricultural improvement is exceeding the rates of population growth. These are very short-term projections and we do not know how long this can go on; and of course there are other issues which we have to take in to account. We have to consider changing standards particularly those which demand types of food which are more costly in terms of production. We ought also to cast an eye on our obligations to the hungry under-developed world. Two points we ought to make are first that although it is perfectly true that the rate we are taking land for urban purposes is now less than it was in the 1930s, it is still twice the rate at which land is being taken in the United States. We are taking one per cent of our land resources per annum while they are taking one half of one per cent. The second point of course is that this demand in the United States is evenly distributed whereas urban land is 7 per cent of the total land surface of Great Britain and 23 per cent of the south-east region. On present population projections we shall have 11 per cent of Great Britain urbanized by 2000, and 36 per cent of the south-east. It is this question of uneven distribution which simply is not a matter of loss of agricultural production in the direct sense of taking land which is at present producing food.

There are also all sorts of indirect effects. The effect of restraint of agricultural production through the presence of large numbers of non-agricultural people. We know from a lot of interesting work that is going on now of the impact (and this again ties up with this continuity between all settlements) of people moving into agriculture, part timers, hobby farmers, and the like. A much larger area around our urban centres is only semi-agricultural.

V. Z. NEWCOMBE

I would like to give support to some underlying groups of passages in the three papers which said that we should approach our development and planning problems without preconceived ideas. This certainly would apply to the problem of densities which Professor Emrys Jones refers to. Density must be based on function not statistics. It is true that perhaps in earlier plans, densities were based on hunches.

Maybe that was necessary at the time because we all are aware than certain solutions had to be found quickly. We are aware of our short-comings yet plans must be made. I think many of us would agree, that plans which are not perfect are better than no plans at all. In fact one might even say that whatever little progress has been made is perhaps not taken sufficient notice of. There is a gap between research and technology in other fields and there is one suspects, also in planning. Therefore anything which adds a classification, seems to me dangerous perhaps because it would support an approach based on preconceived ideas.

I am not sure to what extent it is at all useful to classify urbanization. What does it matter whether people live in settlements which are urban or which are not urban. I think that in Yugoslavia, for instance, a town is a town if it has more than ten thousand people, and if more than 75 per cent of the population are in so-called urban employment. What does it matter, if each country for this sort of statistical purpose is likely to have a different specification? Some countries – I have heard of an instance in Venezuela – seem to have a sudden increase in urbanization but when one analyses it, it is entirely due to a change in specification as to what is 'urban' as defined by the Registrar General. To emphasize my point, it would be much more appropriate to say that so many people live in settlements of less than two thousand people, so many in this, five or ten thousand, without bothering whether urban or rural or anything else.

Similarly I would ask if classification of settlement patterns is relevant particularly here in the Western World. It may be interesting as a historic study but does it help us in formulating our ideas. Might it not prevent us from thinking without inhibitions? Is it not more important to talk of patterns of industrial location? This industrial location and linkage, seem to me to be increasing in importance and are all necessary for the country to exist and survive. Nothing must be done as I see it to disturb industrial linkage and everything must be done to further support that process. I should be not at all surprised if in due course, much of the present policy of dispersal of industry is going to be abandoned. We are after all in competition with other countries. Maybe this form of dispersal leads to methods of production which are uneconomic in relation to production in those countries where these measures are not introduced.

We are building motorways which cost between half a million and one million pounds per mile. Why not accept then motorways as a main basis along which groups of industrial linkage may be spaced? I do not think the actual places where people live is so important a consideration in this age of mobility. In fact, it may be that here in the

Western World we are going back to where we were a few thousand years ago – we have become nomads again. Many of us must have moved or are still moving as part of our careers. We do not take our tents with us any more but we do move provided there is flexible accommodation available without too much in the way of trouble of fees involved with the legal profession. I cannot see why this mobility should not be accepted as one of the considerations of urban growth and industrial linkage.

Approaching things without preconceived ideas certainly applies to those problems which we in the West may have to meet in a so-called developing country. For example, the standard of subsistence is so much lower than anything one would expect is possible. Here we are saying that six people in secondary industry will probably provide a job for one person in tertiary industry. One suspects that the rates in developing countries is the other way round.

GENERAL DISCUSSION

P.E.A. Johnson-Marshall. I would just like to pose a few problems affecting urban growth and settlement location in the United Kingdom. First I would like to pose the problem of apparently irrational patterns of land values in urban development particularly on the immediate periphery of existing urban areas. I think my second problem should be addressed to non-urban geographers; it is the question of what I call the food 'problem'. This causes the necessity for agricultural production in the United Kingdom. How high should we value it? Is it basically an economic matter? Is it basically a strategic matter? My third problem is possibly directed at all the non-designers and I would call this the image problem if you like the place and non-place problem. I do not think there ever is a rational examination carried out in people's minds of the ideal versus the real situation in terms of the levels of services provided for example.

This is linked to the redistribution of population as first proposed in the Barlow Commission. Can we afford the heavy cost of rehabilitation which is necessary to attract people back to the old industrial areas. For example, infra-structure in these areas carries a heavy cost. Also I would ask what the implications are of allowing growth to continue with the eventual lack of space and the almost inevitable lack of environmental qualities. These seem to me to be areas where cost benefit studies could be helpful.

A very quick question to the civil servants on the problems of a major single investment such as a Channel Tunnel, a new airport or a new university, or the major infra-structure of motorways or reservoirs. Should these lead population and industry or follow them?

In my view hitherto the civil servants have tended to allow them to follow rather than lead.

I want to ask of our engineering colleagues the question, can the technological potential be matched by the psychological adjustment in the use of all these new technologies in the fields of telecommunications and rapid transit; for example, can we really use new communication techniques to assist in environmental quality?

C. Blake. I have a very small point but I think nevertheless one of some substance from Dr Thorpe's paper. He quotes figures in evidence for the conclusion that the linkage pattern is now spread over a wider area than those of the past. I suspect that these figures do not in fact bear out this conclusion in quite the way in which he thinks. It is not clear, for instance, whether these figures are intended net or gross inter-regional flows; but what they do obscure and what I think is very important in the study of industrial location are the intra-sectoral flows. These figures are drawn up in the broad industrial categories – of the Standard Industrial Classification.

It is emerging from a survey which we are doing in Dundee, that some of the most important linkages are these intra-sectoral linkages. If you take mechanical engineering for example, the location of their sources of crude metal is not nearly so important as where their final markets for manufactured goods are. What is important, is the facilities for sub-contracting within their own sector and this is one of the great advantages that the Birmingham area has been having with engineering over the West of Scotland. I think the linkages are there and they are still highly important but they can be obscured by this kind of broad input–output analysis.

P. Stone. I would like to raise two points. The first one is the question of the availability of land. I agree here with Professor Emrys Jones that nationally I do not think we should worry too much about this reduction in agricultural land. I think regionally however, the problem is much more important – particularly in regions that are already heavily populated – for two main reasons. They tend to take the land on which productivity is high and increasing fastest and also they need land for recreational activities.

This leads me on to this question of the advantages which industrialists find when they develop in certain regions. I wonder how much work has been done with this so far. Are the advantages to the industrialists outweighed by the disadvantages to the economy as a whole which has to provide the infra-structure?

The other point I wanted to make was about the importance of certain types or urban form. Various shapes and so on have been discussed. I think the point is that these different forms are important in so far as they do affect the systems, the systems of transport, communications, public utility service and so on; we do need at least to know whether there are diseconomies in certain forms of development rather than others.

W.F. Harris. My first comment is on Professor Emrys Jones point about the possibility of being able to tolerate a higher degree of concentration into urban areas if the population had some possibility of getting out into other areas. In a highly industrialized area like Tyneside it is geographically possible but one is faced with the fact that this type of activity is limited by people's horizons which in the vast majority are limited to 'baccy, beer and bingo'.

The next point was mentioned by Professor Bowen Jones who questioned the role of the city as a place of innovation and change. I think it is very essential that the cities in Development Areas that we are trying to revitalize, should be made in to what C.P. Snow would describe as centres of excellence, centres of innovation and change. A characteristic of an area like Tyneside is that the youngsters leave school earlier than anywhere else in the British Isles, they study less in terms of their further education and they develop less in educational terms. Those that do become well-educated, and well-qualified, migrate from the area. They haemorrage their talent and the area is not only left with the old but the relatively untalented, unskilled and untaught. This is a very real problem that the Development Areas are faced with and I wondered if Professor Bowen Jones would comment. How does one identify whether these things that I have been talking about are the cause or the effect of the poverty that has been experienced in the areas. Probably there are other areas and I would rather suspect that the south-west is in very much the same sort of condition. Are these things causes, are they effects or is there a sort of feedback in the mechanism which puts an area in this plight? How can one possibly hope to break it? It is studies into this sort of thing I refer to in my paper when I lament that we can throw a hundred million pounds a year into the very blunt industrial incentives that the government provides without any research being undertaken with very little money devoted towards provision of many much finer tools with which deep incisions could be made into what I believe are far more fundamental problems in the Development Areas.

D. Thorpe. Probably the most important point which I was trying to consider concerns our measurement and our conception of distance. This is all too frequently a physical thing, expanded in terms of x miles when really we ought to be thinking in terms of cost or psychological distance. On Mr Harris's point, the imagination to move is certainly something very important in any settlement system and hence the relevance of my remarks about the lingering on in some of the highly industrialized zones of the nineteenth century of a close integration and a short pychological distance.

To Mr Newcombe, I think on occasions a number of speakers have been unkind to the planner. He is always a nice man to throw something at and I think the reason they are unkind is perhaps rather significant. I think that the planner, in presenting his plan to some extent must have an eye to the dramatic and to some extent that eye is too dramatic certainly in his presentation of his plan, albeit not in his thought process up to the plan. The plan may in fact be based on reality but the way in which he presents it is dramatic in order, quite properly, to get the plan accepted. To some extent therefore we have to scratch and see if it was a good plan.

I fully accept Professor Blake's point that linkages within a particular category may well be important, may probably be more what pattern in the Bristol region would be within categories. I do not know what pattern in the Bristol region would be within categories. It is a pity that Professor Parry Lewis is not here because I suspect that his survey results suggested that in fact the linkages within categories in fact were relatively small. We clearly need far more information and really my point in putting this table forward was to draw attention to the need rather than to say that this was in fact really the substantive illustration.

Bowen-Jones. Mr Harris raised the point on critical size and critical significance. In some ways, in Tyneside, he is talking about firstly the non-appearance of an elite and secondly the disappearance of a potential elite. Both as equally frustrating. In terms of Tyneside one could think that partly this is a matter of relative advantage. Tyneside may not in itself have particular relative advantages upon which we can rapidly build economic opportunity. I would agree entirely to use this as one element in the research into the influence of government policy on expenditure. I regard it as absurd for instance to indulge in spending money in subsidizing Tyneside ship building without establishing the possibility that Tyneside ship building might change economically, technologically, socially and so on.

Emrys Jones. First of all Professor Coppock's important point on the appraisal of the agricultural possibilities and the impact of towns. If one could expand the concept of selective urban development, the regional implications as well as the local implications of using grade one land or grade three are very great. What I wanted to stress, is that the impact of agricultural land is merely one facet and we are not to be excused from looking at all the other facets because we thought of one reason why a town should not expand any further into agricultural land.

Professor Coppock also asked one question which tied up with several other points that have been made. When is a town too big? is a marvellous question, like the title of a recent book on, An Awkward Size for a Town. Well at any point one can say that a town is too big if it ceases to function properly. There is no specific size. If we accept that centrality equals accessability (and this is what we have always depended on since the very first town) then if accessibility ceases to coincide with centrality then this generates considerable problems.

We have some examples of towns in which something has happened to the centrality and new forms have to be thought out. One thinks of forms in the natural world which have grown too big for their function and consequently just disappeared. It is a sobering thought of course that no urban civilization has survived; if you think of all the great urban civilizations, they are all dead except the one we are in. So it would not be surprising if this one is also going to the same end unless we can actually think about changing it. This is what worries me about Mr Saunders' use of the term organic growth. To me organic growth means reproducing the past and this of course ties up with Mr Newcombe who also rejected trends. In other words we are pleased to accept the preconceived ideas. What happens in nature of course is that things do not die out entirely because there are mutations and even if we do accept organic growth is it not time we started to look for mutations. In other words we should experiment with new forms and see what can answer the needs of the present day instead of depending on preconceived ideas and trends and so on to solve our problem for us.

We tend to think of Britain and even cities as closed systems. Even Britain is not a closed system, there is worldwide movement which I think represents geographical determinisms. Of my own background, Wales has always had not a non-urban realm but a rural non-class realm. Not only did Wales have no towns but Wales had no villages. The people appeared to be isolated in the woods. No one however is less isolated than the Welshman in his detached little cottage. The whole rural fabric of Wales depends on this inter-relationship from one spot to the other so that even the biggest thing we can muster up, the Eistedfodd, moves from one town to another quite regularly. This is why we did not have a capital city until about ten years ago. Wherever the Eistedfodd happened to be was the capital for that year. Here is one of those many mutations which I think one should play around with. If we can free ourselves from the model which has really by now, become so much of a dinosaur that it is in danger of killing itself, then we should have alternatives for the future which we could look forward to quite hopefully.

Part Four . Politics

British Politics and the two Regionalisms
L. J. Sharpe, Fellow of Nuffield College, Oxford

Urban Planning and Local Government
W. F. Harris, Principal City Officer, Newcastle upon Tyne

Discussion :
D. Lyddon, Scottish Development Department
J. Cornford, Professor of Politics, University of Edinburgh
J. Erickson, Professor of Politics, University of Edinburgh

British Politics and the Two Regionalisms

L. J. SHARPE

For the last five years or so regionalism has been an important political talking point in this country, especially since the establishment of the regional economic planning machinery in December 1964. This paper is largely concerned with this institutional aspect of regionalism rather than the intellectual history of the various concepts, although these are touched on from time to time.

Like all issues which achieve a fairly wide degree of popularity, discussion seems to have got diffuse and a little confused. For some people it would seem, regionalism is just another aspect of fairly rudimentary notions that greater scale brings economic benefits; or that our old friend – that Stakhanovite of the reform front – the internal combustion engine, has enabled people to enjoy more spacious living patterns. In both cases larger areas of administration are demanded and these may be dubbed as different facets of the efficiency school. To put it crudely, a fairly common view of regionalism may be paraphrased as favouring any area of operation provided that it is wider than any existing area. For others a third element is ushered into the discussion, namely, the decentralization of power. Regionalism becomes a synonym for a brand of quasifederalism and as such is seen as a way of reforming local government, promoting economic growth and, more recently, appeasing Scottish and Welsh nationalism.

For this school not only is a regional structure seen as a way of achieving greater efficiency but also greater popular participation in the process of government as well. And it is perhaps here that there is the greatest need for careful clarification of concepts since there is an implicit assumption that there is no conflict between these objectives, that all roads lead conveniently to Rome. To what extent those who want greater participation and greater efficiency are pursuing a chimera need not detain us since it is only one among many regional proposals. At the heart of the ambiguities and general muzziness which surrounds the whole subject is the central fact that there are two distinct though linked forms of regionalism which have fundamentally different origins and seek to serve very different and to some extent conflicting purposes. [1]

Without putting too sharp an emphasis on what was necessarily a haphazard and spasmodic process, a useful starting point in disentangling the two forms is to trace their origins. The first form of regionalism is one of a number of alternatives that have been put forward for modernizing local government. As we shall see it has also influenced central policy-making and some non-local government administrative arrangements, but its essential feature is that it is primarily concerned with local government and in this sense may be termed regionalism from below or *decentralist regionalism*. This has had a fairly long history[2] and the common thread has been that local government boundaries are inadequate and ought to be redrawn so as to conform more closely to the physical, cultural or socio-economic regions of the country. The emphasis has changed over the years; currently most emphasis is placed on socio-geographic considerations, but all three have held sway at various periods.

Without over-emphasizing continuity it is possible to see the origins of this school of thought in a remarkably prescient lecture given by H. G. Wells to the Fabian Society in 1902 [3]. This was taken up by the Society in the new Heptarchy proposals and echoed in the writings of the geographers Fawcett and Mackinder and of G. D. H. Cole following the First World War. It also found practical expression in the London regional plans of Unwin in the early 1930s and during the 1940s in the various advisory regional plans of which Abercrombie's Greater London Plan is the best known. Post-war new towns, expanded towns and the green-belt policy, are all off-shoots to a greater or lesser degree from this concept of regionalism. It is also apparent in the post Second World War writings of G. D. H. Cole, Peter Self and W. A. Robson. But in all three special emphasis is given to the question of redesigning the local government of the conurbations and their immediate hinterlands. Here, and in the advisory plans, it is possible to detect an important shift in emphasis. This is towards the special needs of physical planning and cognate services in the major urban concentrations and away from devising a pattern of areas over the country as a whole for providing mainly the public utility services.

More recently the decentralist regional approach has been given a new lease of life with the Concept of the City region devised by Maurice Ash and Derek Senior. [4] Particularly the latter who takes the city region as a framework for an ingenious new pattern for local government. The basis of this region is not the broad physical and cultural unities of the earlier concepts but the smaller socio-economic concept of the third order service centre and its hinterland.

This shift from the broad region with largely physically determined boundaries – Wells wanted a single authority for public utility services for the whole of the Thames basin – to major urban agglomerations and finally to the third order centres, not only reflects greater theoretical sophistication but also the changes that have been wrought or are thought likely to be wrought in our pattern of life by better communications and greater personal mobility. It also reflects the weakening of the public utility element in the regional concept following the nationalisation of national highways, gas, electricity and the hospitals. Although it is interesting to note the varying degrees of homage that were paid to the broader pre-war regional concepts in the administrative machinery created for providing these services. The city region concept too harks back to the earlier doctrine by arguing that at least some of the nationalized services ought to be returned to local government if it were constituted on a city regional basis. The city regional approach is probably better suited to some of the services which are not the responsibility or local government than to some that are.

Here one sees the persistent intertwining of two aspects of decentralist regionalism in all its forms. First there is the insistence that local government boundaries should follow what are claimed to be definable geographic boundaries whether they are physical, demographic or socio-economic. Second, that they should circumscribe units which in terms of population and resources were adequate for the services to be provided. For town planning and related services the geographic and service requirements may coincide, but for other services it may not, particularly if considerations of what may be called democratic viability are also taken into account. Since the object is to improve the structure of local government it is difficult to see how they could be entirely excluded. It is for these reasons that geographic factors can never be the sole consideration although this is not always made as apparent as it might be.

The second type of regionalism has a more recent history and has been primarily concerned with improving the effectiveness of central government in the national economy by means of regional agencies. In this sense it may be described as regionalism from above or *centralist regionalism*.

The Special Areas Act of 1934 marks the beginning of this approach. This Act was designed to combat the problems arising from high structural unemployment in certain areas such as West Cumberland, South Wales and the Clyde basin, by attracting new industry into these areas. Regional Commissioners were appointed – one for England and Wales and one for Scotland – to undertake the task of attracting new industry to these by means of special concessions and monetary incentives. [5] In 1940 the Barlow Commission, whose report embraced both types of regionalism, underlined the need to look at the geographic unbalance in the economy that had emerged since the first world war on a regional basis.

The war also spawned new regional machinery in the form of Regional Commissioners who were charged with the coordination of civil defence for each of the regions in the event of invasion. Regional Production Boards were also set up composed of civil servants and industrialists to coordinate the activities of the Ministries of Aircraft Production, Supply, Labour, Transport and the Board of Trade with the object of raising the level of industrial production. After the war both the pre-war and war-time Regional Commissioners and other regional agencies disappeared except for the Regional Production Boards which survived in the form of Regional Boards for Industry with purely advisory functions. Some Departments also had established their own regional controllers with a general oversight for departmental responsibility within each region, notably Transport and Power, but these disappeared after the war. Some Departments retained their own regional machinery which had been set up to meet war-time and immediate post-war conditions. There was a degree of rationalisation after the war but by the mid-1950s much of this had been wound up. An important Departmental regional system was created for town planning under the Ministry of Housing and Local Government. The last remnant of this arrangement did not finally disappear until 1958.

The next phase in the evolution of centralist regionalism began, so far as it is possible to pin-point it, with the high levels of unemployment in early 1963 in Scotland, Merseyside and the North-East. This was dangerously close to a general election. Special investment programmes were started to stimulate employment in these areas and a Cabinet Minister Mr Quintin Hogg, headed a special study of the North-East. Scotland already had an effective instrument for making such a study in the shape of the Development Department which was set up in the preceding year. A step in the direction of a similar Department for England and Wales was taken when Mr Heath had the job of Secretary of State for Industry, Trade and Regional Development added to that of President of the Board of Trade when he took up that office in late 1963.

In policy terms, the appearance of the two growth programmes for Scotland and the North-East is also important since they introduced on to the political stage the regional approach to employment policy. This approach is distinctive because it placed emphasis on the importance of growth points. This concept had first been spelled out in the Toothill Report on the Scottish economy in 1961 and refers to areas where new industry seemed to have the best chance of taking root, rather than any area with a relatively high unemployment rate. The other element in the new regional approach was the recognition that unemployment policy should take account of the quality of the regional environment or infra-structure, that relocation of industry demanded something more than lower factory rents and financial incentives. But if communications and power supplies, housing and schools were to be improved then the activities of these central departments whose responsibilities these were had to be coordinated. There was a complete reversal of the retreat from planning which began in 1952 and had culminated in the Local Employment Act in 1960. Henceforth economic planning could neither be reduced to mopping up pockets of unemployment nor could it remain the province of one Department.

Perhaps more decisive was the National Economic Development Council's report which also appeared in 1963 : *Conditions Favourable to Faster Growth*. This established the vital link between unemployment policy and national economic growth. Tackling unemployment ceased to be largely an ameliorative, equalitarian activity and was established as an essential feature of successful national economic management. Helping the developing areas was not just another example of misplaced social welfare that was sapping our economic growth but an essential prerequisite for achieving more rapid growth than before. Redistributive justice and economic efficiency were happily joined. And faster growth it must be remembered had the additional political attraction of providing a larger slice of the national cake for the public sector without any increase in general taxation. The stage was clearly set for the reorientation of national economic planning in a regional direction. This came with the new Labour government in 1964, taking the form of the regional planning boards and planning councils under the new economic planning departments, the Department of Economic Affairs.

It is not necessary for the purposes of this paper to give an account of this new system, the respective responsibilities of the boards and councils, their relationship with the D.E.A. and the defunct National Plan which emerged a year later. The essential point to note is that this second tradition of centralist regionalism not only differs from the decentralist variety in its historical origins, but seeks to serve very different purposes. Let us look more clearly at what precisely these purposes are and how they differ from those of decentralist regionalism.

As we have seen, there were particular factors which precipitated the emergence of the new regional machinery in 1964, to which ought to be added the very important and purely political factors associated with a new administration's legitimate desire to strike out in new directions and to the no less legitimate need to accommodate competing demands for high office among the party leadership. But at the broadest level, the centralist tradition as it emerged in the new regional planning machinery, is the logical corollary to the ineluctable tightening of the central government's grip on the overall management of an economy which has shown itself, since 1945, to be in almost perpetual crisis.

More precisely, the new regional economic planning arose out of the realization that a fast rate of growth of the total economy could only be achieved if the use of the manpower and capital resources in each region was centrally planned so as to minimize the diseconomies arising from the maldistribution of new and declining industry between the regions; the maldistribution of unemployment and under-employment; and the lack of any framework which linked the investment programmes of Central Departments, local authorities and public corporations within regions in relation to some kind of overall efficiency goal.

Here we see in plainest terms the fundamental distinction between the two concepts of regionalism. Whereas decentralist regionalism is largely concerned with providing a better framework in which elected bodies with their own sources of revenue can carry out their functions, centralist regionalism had become by the early 1960s, if anything, even more concerned with making central government more effective. For the overriding purpose of regional planning became that of re-distributing economic resources between the regions. Some regions stand to gain from this process in that they will get more than they would have got were there no planning. But equally some regions must lose, growth or no growth. This process requires that there is some higher common superior to do the re-distributing. In a nutshell, centralist regionalism is an instrument for strengthening central government whereas decentralist regionalism has sought to strengthen local government. [5] This means that the two concepts cannot be rolled up into a single brand new system which will banish the ills of the economy, those of local government as well and provide Wales and Scotland with a quasi-federal status.

The function of local government above all else is to cultivate its own patch. No elected regional body raising a sizable slice of its own resources and carrying out a range of executive functions could be asked to form part of a centralist regional system if one of its primary purposes was to be the instrument whereby resources were diverted to another region. This is not even to touch on the problem of who decides, and on what basis, which region will be the gainers and which the losers. Any doubts that this is a problem are dispelled by a glance at the reports of the present regional planning councils, their public pronouncements, or their evidence to the Hunt Committee. The Northern Council casts envious eyes at the flow of public investment across the Tweed. Likewise, Yorks and Humberside and the South-West watch impatiently the similar flow to the Northern region. Meanwhile the South-East expostulates on the stupidity of siphoning off industry or diverting resources from its region which it sees as the only goose in the yard that lays the golden eggs. These are merely appointed advisory bodies made up for the most part of nonpoliticians. Where vital interests are concerned representative bodies represent. Experience has been much the same in the creation of regional economic advisory bodies in France.

This is not to say that the two regionalisms have no connection with each other. So long as local authorities remain responsible for land use planning they must be involved in the new style regional economic planning. Land use planning and economic planning are now recognized as being merely different facets and different *stages* of the total planning process. Like the happy conjunction of traditional ameliorative employment policy with economic growth policy, this was a very important intellectual break-through. For the essence of *regional* economic planning is that it has a vital spatial component. Economic planning must involve consideration of alternative spatial arrangements of capital investment on the ground, i.e. land use planning. One of the key factors is communications. Specialization of land use implies some form of linkage between the different specialisms and adequate links are just as important on economic as on any other grounds.

It might be thought that this synthesis came a little late in the day. But it seems to have come late to most countries although there were perhaps particular difficulties inhibiting its emergence in Britain. There was the traditional lack of interest by economists in locational economics which was largely left to the geographers. Equally there was the distrust of orthodox economic theory by town planners. It is no exaggeration to say that they saw one of the functions of town planning as putting right the aesthetic and social harm created by the unrestrained application of orthodox economic theories in the past. [6] The fact that industrial location policy and land use planning has always been the responsibility of separate and therefore rival Departments in Whitehall, should not be overlooked as another important contributory factor to the division between the two types of planning. Another factor was the lack of forward thinking in Whitehall about capital investment for public services which impinge on development for which it was responsible. It was not until the late 1950s and early 1960s that investment programmes were drawn up for motorways, railways, hospitals and the universities. [7] Town planners could hardly take account of what did not exist, however strong their predelictions were for town form rather than the price mechanism.

The marrying of the two aspects of planning does not itself presuppose a single authority. The need for a new local government structure does not begin nor end with land use planning. Local government is responsible for other major services. Planning is one of local government's most important services and is likely to grow in importance as usable land gets scarcer in the areas of major population concentration. But it is only one among others and derives its effectiveness from the fact that it is joined with other services – highways, traffic management, main drainage, housing, education – at the operational level. Each may demand a different scale for effective provision so that if they are to remain together no single service can have an optimum area of operation.

We are, it must be admitted, something less than crystal clear about what economic planning in regional terms means operationally. As a definable activity it is in its infancy. It would be misguided to mistake good intentions and wishful guesses for the reality of an administrative machine and a professional staff with a clear executive task. It would be an even bigger mistake to make its supposed demands the basis of a new quasi federal pattern of government. There are in any case fairly firm grounds for thinking there is no need to.

The new town planning processes and techniques that will be ushered in under the 1968 Town Planning Act will amongst other things provide a new economic dimension to traditional land use planning and give communications their rightful place. It is therefore a reasonable assumption, to put it no higher, to suppose that the new style town planning can be keyed in to regional economic plans so that the broad division of responsibilities that must exist between locally elected autonomous bodies and a central government committed to national economic management may continue. This is certainly how the Planning Advisory Group, on whose report the new Act is based, saw the relationship between the two aspects of planning. The link would be the new structure policy plans drawn up by local authorities. In this way land-use planning as embodied in the local and action area plans would form part of a continuous chain of planning decisions right up to the regional, and one supposes, another National Plan. Clearly there would need to be some firmly established machinery for bringing local planning authorities into a much closer association with the regional economic planning machine so that the two elements in planning at the regional level can be enmeshed. This was also envisaged in the PAG Report. [8]

Precisely how this can be done lies outside the ambit of this paper and obviously must depend, amongst other things, on what pattern of local government emerges following the reports of the royal commissions on local government in England and Scotland. Whatever form the link takes it will bristle with difficulties. As we have seen, not least of the difficulties will be that any kind of representative regional body must develop an allegiance to its region which cuts across the very basis of effective regionalized national planning.

Of course it is quite possible for economic planning to slowly bow out of the political arena as it did in the 1950s. The present fairly wide agreement on the need for planning should not disguise the fact that it still retains powerful ideological undertones and could well come under fire with a change of government. Its future is also rather less secure if the present ambiguous regional planning machinery continues and if our rate of economic growth continues at its present sluggish rate. A static economy has, after all, far less to plan. However, the future of economic planning is not the only factor which will determine whether we continue to have some kind of regional machinery. There are other possibly more decisive factors at work. They are of two kinds, the first are what may be called functional, the second political.

The functional arise from the peculiar structure of government in Britain. We are possibly unique among the advanced industrial democracies in not having an intermediate tier of government between central and local government. Northern Ireland is in a special category, with a high degree of autonomy but short of federal status, and Scotland and Wales have their own devolved 'Offices', each under a Secretary of State. The latter now has its own representative council as well. But until the appearance of the regional planning boards. England with its population of 43 million, has had no tier of government catering for those aspects of government that have a narrower ambit than the nation as a whole yet are not purely local in character or scope. Federal systems have them by definition and most of the remaining great industrial democracies follow with variations the French prefectoral pattern. This involves the interposition of an agent of central government responsible for the general oversight of central government services for an area wider than individual local authorities. This agent also reflects back to the centre the particular interests and problems of the locality he covers. To put it another way, England had no generalist agency responsible for the whole range of public services nearer to the actual field of operations than the Cabinet, or interdepartmental committee.

This has meant that central administration has suffered two important defects. It is top heavy and it lacks coordination in the field. It has become top heavy as functions have been progressively added statute by statute without the possibility of properly distinguishing these indisputable national functions, which only central government can undertake, and those which could be devolved on to agencies lower down the administrative line.

The consequences of this process are not merely that central departments are overloaded, but also that central government is unable to get on with those vital jobs which only it can do. If there is a kind of Gresham's Law for general administration whereby the day-to-day routine work always drives out the more complex long term stuff, so too the traditional controlling, regulating and inspecting functions of British central departments seem always to gain precedence over the formulation of the broad forward policies which should precede the exercise of the controlling and regulating functions. Thus in the field of town and country planning the central government has been so busy approving development plans and their five-yearly revisions, processing planning appeals and exercising call-in powers that it has never had time to produce the national land-use plan which should have logically underpinned its decisions on individual development plans. Similarly, in the field of transport any notion of a total view of national communications has until recently languished in the shade of the vast bureaucratic tree that is required to maintain close control of highway maintenance and traffic management.

The second functional aspect which demands some kind of regional treatment – the lack of coordination nearer to the field of operations than Whitehall – is the more important. Overloading can be mitigated at a pinch by devolution within the present vertical departmental pattern, without the creation of a horizontal generalist tier at regional level. This is not mere academic theorizing, it is already being done. Recent transport legislation and the New Town Act establish various devices for achieving it including ad hoc agencies (Passenger Transport Authorities), more autonomy for local authorities (local plans and traffic regulations) and discretionary power to inspectors for planning enquiries.

Coordination is more important in the context of this paper because it cannot be achieved without an intermediate tier. It is also a fundamental prerequisite of regional planning which requires as a minimum that the public investment programmes of all the major public agencies – central, local, public corporation – within a region be related to each other. But the need for coordination is wider than this and relates to the whole spectrum of public services. Without the intermediate level we lack an agency for appraising the total effect of public policy within a region and for assessing how the different departmental strands of that policy inter-relate.

At the fairly abstract level the need for an intermediate tier is derived from the need to look at government responsibilities in two ways. Not merely vertically function by function but also horizontally within specified areas at less than the national level. Specialization by function is a necessary and vital element in modern administrative arrangements as it is in other activities, but the 'education service', the 'electricity industry' or the 'health service' are in a sense abstractions. The reality which must also be taken into account is that a particular 'service' is composed of many component parts distributed over the country with wide variations in the quality of these components, the demands made on them and the general context in which they operate. It is this horizontal or area focus that local government provides. But there is now a wider range of public services which fall for different reasons outside local government.

This long-term secular need for a regional level of government is linked to the first of the political factors which seems likely to sustain a regional dimension in British politics whatever happens in the short run to economic planning. This is the steady growth in popular pressure for equality of opportunity. In most industrial democracies the electorate seems increasingly less willing to tolerate wide variations between regions in what are called life changes – job opportunities, educational opportunities, the quality of the environment and so forth. This is the spatial facet of relative deprivation. Although this variation between regions has probably been exaggerated and is substantially less in Britain than in, say, Italy or France, [9] a sense of deprivation exists and has grown in strength over the past five years or so. It began mainly round the theme of the differences between North and South, but now has developed a regional refinement. If we assume that the polarization of industry within the economy, which seems to be a characteristic of many other industrial countries, continues then the grounds for this sense of relative deprivation is likely to grow rather than diminish. [10]

Without a regional level of government the responsibility for overall local interests – the job that was noted earlier of appraising the total effect of public policy within a region – has been left to local authorities or to M.P.s. Neither, in the nature of things, is equipped for the job. Leaving aside the probability of some bias in favour of the South-East by a permanently London-based higher bureaucracy, [11] the absence of a regional tier has meant that investment policies for individual services have been pursued on the basis of undoubtedly equitable criteria and formulae, yet the end result could appear to be inequitable. New motorways may have been built where traffic was densest, subsidized factories where unemployment was highest, railway lines or coal mines closed that make the heaviest losses and so on; but these policies may *add up* to apparent and palpable discrimination in particular areas. The creation of representative regional councils in some regions may have only served to sharpen the focus of the discontent which the absence of a regional 'eye' has generated.

It seems doubtful though that regional sentiment is rooted only in the sense of relative deprivation. It may, for example, be to some extent another manifestation of the slow crumbling of social attitudes. As W. J. M. Mackenzie has pointed out, [12] geographic position and social class position often go hand in hand. Certainly in the North versus South discussions it is sometimes difficult to disentangle social class aspects from geographical aspects. It also seems likely that the emergence of regional sentiment appears to be greater than it really is because the rightly celebrated homogeneity of our society was until recently an unquestioned intellectual orthodoxy which masked a true understanding of substantial variation between different parts of the country. It is doubtful whether we were ever as uniform in our attitudes or as centralized in our tastes as some of the theorizing in the late 1950s suggested, whether the subject was voting behaviour, the future of provincial culture or changes in working-class patterns of life.

It also seems likely that the growth of new regional sentiment has been spontaneous. At this stage in its development it is difficult to pin it down or to trace all its causes, even supposing they exist. The main point is that it exists and whatever its origins has evoked a fascinating catalogue of responses ranging from the setting up of the Hunt Committee to the BBC's experiment of substituting Australians for traditional southern English announcers. Wilfred Pickles has not yet been called back to fill his war-time role as news reader but the success of 'Z Cars', 'Coronation Street', even the slightly improbable concept of 'Swinging Newcastle' all in their way reflect the break-up of metropolitan dominance. Who would have imagined ten short years ago that Liverpool would have chic? There is no reason to suppose that this vague generalised upsurge of regional loyalty with its strong undercurrent of anti-metropolitan feeling won't continue to exert an important though possibly indirect influence on the future of regionalism.

These other less tangible aspects have taken us some way from relative deprivation but they do serve to remind us that account must be taken of a complexity of factors and that too much emphasis must not be placed on the inadequacy of the administrative machine as a source of the new regional sentiment. After all Scotland has had its own sub-government, the Scottish Office, for some time, and in its Development Department has the machinery for the kind of integrated appraisal of the economic aspects of public policy that were seen to be lacking in the English regions. Yet it would be difficult to argue that Scotland had escaped a feeling of relative deprivation. In this instance we need to examine another political factor which seems likely to exert a powerful influence on the development of regional forms of government in this country. This is the cultural nationalism that has emerged so suddenly in Scotland and to a lesser extent in Wales. It is this suddenness which must make any discussion of its origins highly speculative and predictions about its future development even more so. Most of the factors nonetheless that have already been discussed which have generated the new regional consciousness probably apply for Scotland and Wales. The difference seems to be that there are additional historical and cultural pegs on which to hang the case and therefore suggest that devolution is likely to go a lot further. There may be other developments which reinforce this likelihood.

The first is the erosion of political homogeneity in Britain. Again predictions are dangerous but there are some fairly strong indicators. If the extent of homogeneity in general in this country has been exaggerated, political homogeneity has nevertheless existed. The unifying factor is social class which seemed to cut across most of the other personal characteristics of voters such as sex, age and religion. But it is plausible to assume that the rise of Scottish nationalism, if not Welsh, is a reflection of the weakening of the social class factor. One reason for this could be that with Britain's standing in the world on the decline there may be less attraction for the Scottish elector in identifying himself with the country as a whole rather than Scotland itself, to identify with fellow Scotsmen rather than fellow manual workers or fellow professional people. Disenchantment with the existing parties seems to have been accelerated by the apparent failure of the first major change of government for over a decade to have any effect on our economic situation or power to influence events abroad. It certainly seems plausible to assume that frustration with the

Labour party would be more likely to find expression outside the Conservative party which has been in steady decline throughout Wales and Scotland for a number of years. As the name under which they fight in Scotland denotes, the Conservatives have been the English party in a sense which the Labour party never have.

The attractions and possibilities of becoming a new state are certainly greater than ever before. Eire has pointed the way whereby the internal tax system can be manipulated so as to entice foot-loose capital on the look-out for cheap skilled and semi-skilled labour within reasonable distance of big international markets. But this is an aspect which makes independence feasible for some small, comparatively well-favoured states, it hardly explains the undoubted persistence of nationalism as a world-wide phenomenon. De-colonization and the creation of the United Nations seem to have been the important elements in sustaining nationalism since the end of the Second World War.

The UN itself by offering a loose framework of order in international affairs, a forum for mobilizing diplomatic pressure outside the ambit of the great powers, and agencies for providing aid, has made independence for small communities more attractive than it ever was in the past. Most of the member States of the UN have a smaller population than Scotland.

Viewed against this international background our surprise at the emergence of Scottish and Welsh nationalism seems a little insular. The abnormal emphasis on economic factors in most general discussion of British politics in recent years may have perhaps made us the prisoners of two experiences, the American and the Russian. There are grounds for viewing the USA and the USSR as the last of the great nineteenth-century empires as much as prototypes for the future. We have assumed too glibly that the future always lies with the larger unit. This was abundantly evident during the debate on whether we should join the Common Market. It ought not perhaps to need underlining in a country which has to import most of its raw materials and half of its food that it is political rather than economic factors which determine the creation of states. Our failure to establish enduring larger units out of hitherto separate entities, beginning with the Central African Federation, followed by the abortive West Indian Federation and the slow crumbling of the Malaysian and the Nigerian, are both sufficient testament to this and to our weakness for larger units. Even two of the older federations we have established – the Indian and the Canadian – are now under severe pressure from cultural nationalism.

Again a note of caution must be struck, prediction in politics is usually futile. The very rapidity of the rise of cultural nationalism in Britain means that it could decline just as rapidly. International trends may or may not be a guide, they certainly do not show that Scotland, still less Wales, will inevitably hive themselves off from the United Kingdom. Nor is it the purpose of this paper to suggest that they should. But it is important to remind ourselves that some of the forces which impinge in the regional debate here may have links with trends in the rest of the world and that in these trends the tendencies for separation are just as strong as those for cohesion.

One final point. There are clearly links but there is also conflict between the aims of Scottish and Welsh nationalism and much of the discussion in this paper about regionalism. The logic of cultural nationalism is not the creation of regional bodies in England but of a more self-conscious and more unified England. We must be careful in other words to distinguish sentiment from other arguments for a regional system. If there is a case for dividing up England on regional lines then there is an equally strong case for dividing up Wales and Scotland. The objective differences between North and South Wales are greater than those between the East and West Midlands, or between the South-East and East Anglia. Similarly there is nothing in the whole of Central and Southern England to compare with the socio-economic differences that exist between Central Scotland and the Highlands and Islands. The logic of regionalism, as some of the Common Market ideologists are aware, is inimical to the logic of nationalism.

REFERENCES

1. See L. J. Sharpe, 'Regionalism in Great Britain' in *Die Verwaltungsregion*; Schriftenriene des Vereins für Kommunalwissen-schaften, Kohlhammer, Berlin, 1967.
2. See the invaluable B. C. Smith, *Regionalism in England No.2: Its Purpose, 1905–1965* Acton Society Trust, 1965. Also a useful summary of regional planning in Britain is given in P. Self, 'Regional Planning in Britain: Analysis and Evolution', *Regional Studies*, Vol. 1, No. 1, May 1967.
3. H. G. Wells, 'A Paper on Administrative Areas read before the Fabian Society', originally published in *Mankind in the Making* (London, 1903) and republished in A. Maass (ed.), *Area and Power* (Michigan, 1959).
4. M. Ash, *The Human Cloud*. Town and Country Planning Association, 1962; D. Senior, *Regional Planning and Democracy*, paper to the T.C.P.A. National Conference, 1964; D. Senior, 'The City Region

as an Administrative Unit', *Political Quarterly*, Spring 1965;
P. Senior (ed.), *Regional City*, Longmans, 1966.

5.   That the creation of regional machinery can mean the tightening
of central control has been pointed out by J. W. Fesler in
'Approaches to the Understanding of Decentralization', *The
Journal of Politics*, Vol. 27, 1965. For a masterly discussion of the
basic problems underlying regional administration see the same
author's *Area and Administration*, University of Alabama Press,
1949.

6.   D. Foley, 'British Town Planning : One Ideology or Three ?',
British Journal of Sociology, Vol. 11, No. 3, 1960.

7.   Phipps Turnbull, *Regional Economic Councils and Boards*, address to
the Town Planning Institute, January 1967.

8.   *The Future of Development Plans*, report of the Planning Advisory
Group, H.M.S.O., p 10, para 1 : 44.

9.   D. Eversley, 'North-South Exaggerations', *New Society*, 2nd May
1968.

10.   P. B. M. Jones, 'The Organization of Regional Economic Planning
in France', *Public Administration*, Winter 1967.

11.   J. A. G. Griffith, *Central Departments and Local Authorities*, Allen &
Unwin, 1966.

12.   W. J. M. Mackenzie, *Theories of Local Government*, Greater London
Paper, No. 3, London School of Economics, 1961.

Urban Planning and Local Government

W. F. HARRIS

I feel a bit of a fraud in this academic environment where, quite clearly, one is expected to pull the strands of one's experience together and weave some sort of theory or conclusion about what one had done or what one should be doing.

I have not done that and all I have to offer are a few passing thoughts about some of the practical problems and difficulties that one runs into in the role of an administrator in local government. I do this because I think it has bearing on the subject of urban growth. The mechanism for implementing urban growth or urban contraction for that matter is the mechanism of local government. This is where the initiative starts and this is where the day-by-day decisions have to be made and things have actually to be done and bricks built one on top of another. This is the heart of local government work.

Perhaps I had better make it clear in the first place that I come to local government basically with the eye of an industrialist which is probably not the best sort of eye with which to look at it. It gives one a certain bias, a certain number of preconceived notions, and invariably when I comment on what we are doing or I look at problems in local government, I tend to use industrial experiences as a yard stick rather than some probably better yard stick.

Secondly, I think it is necessary to declare what I mean by the job of local government, in a very simple and generalized fashion. It is to provide the environment and services within our available resources so that people can live their lives to the fullest and can exploit their potential. I see it very simply as that. I do not see it (as probably most of my professional colleagues in other cities would see it) as being the task of complying with certain stipulated pieces of legislation.

One of the main problems of local government is the grass roots problems of how it gets there, i.e. how it gets appointed and what the electorate does about it. The rather sad answer to this is that the electorate does not do very much about it at all. Only about a third of the electorate turns up to vote, and on any real major issues in a city, very seldom does more than a very minute fraction of the percentage of the population express their view or participate : few for example write letters to the paper and even less attend council meetings which of course are usually open to the public. The participation of the public is virtually non-existent and when they do participate in terms of voting it is not the local issues that determine the voting. The consitution of local authorities in all the urban areas is almost invariably conditioned by national politics. It seems to be a peculiarly English habit that we elect a government and within a year or so we then go and elect local governments all over the country of exactly the opposite colour.

The electorate does not respond very well to things that the local authority does. The largest local influence on the electorate is what happens in terms of council house rents and council house building. This is the thing that seems to have most impact on votes – at least what politicians think has most impact on votes. Rates come a very poor second and I have not seen much evidence that sharp increases in rates cause a rejection of any particular representation on local government, or that decreases in rates improve the popularity of the party that is responsible for them.

Another fundamental problem with local governments is the fact that it has to work through committees. Obviously you cannot have a deliberative or decision-taking body of eighty people (more than eighty in some of the bigger cities) taking decisions. Committee work is the only way in which it is legal for local government to delegate its job into manageable hunks for the work actually to be done.

Committee work is a most unsatisfactory way of transacting business in many respects. Committees have no continuity or singleness of mind; they are a group of people each of whom has his own individual ideas and his own individual opinions. There is no compulsive responsibility resting on any individual member. A committee tends therefore to be less responsible than a single executive would be. This is in the very nature of committees. It does not matter whether they are elected representatives or whether they are appointed as a committee in some of your professional institutions.

If you have fifteen people jointly responsible for taking a decision, no one of them feels the responsibility which he feels if he were an executive in industrial or commercial work. Committees cannot communicate with each other. The sort of thing that happens is that if Committee A wants to do something which affects Committee B, it needs Committee B to cooperate with it; then it passes a resolution that it wants Committee B to do something. Later Committee B disagrees. This news reaches Committee A and they resolve that they would like to talk to Committee B so they appoint a delegation and send a request for talks to Committee B who get this still later again.

This goes on and much time can easily be wasted trying to have a dialogue between two committees. It is not a good way of hammering out problems and coming to sound decisions, in reasonable time.

It can be demonstrated mathematically that the very nature of committee voting makes it liable to inconsistency. Each member of a committee can vote logically and sensibly, and yet the end decision of the Committee can be illogical and incoherent.

Officers try not to let this sort of thing happen, by trying to guide and steer the committees; often however, they have to stop action taking place on committee decisions and arrange to take such decisions back so that they can be put right. These are awkward things to do; it is very difficult to get committees to come together and you cannot do it with the same ease as you can with two individuals.

Another aspect of local government work which has its disadvantages stems from the fact that it is based so much on the law. It is legally orientated rather than opportunistically orientated. When a problem arises there is a general tendency to ask what the extent of the powers amount to. Of course in industry and commerce you never ask this question at senior level. There is very considerable freedom of action ; the opportunities are identified and then evaluated. The local government administration has to live with the doctrine of *ultra vires* – in other words he cannot do anything unless there is a law laid down somewhere saying he can do it or he must do it. To a large extent this inhibits the taking of risks. In many decisions in local government risks should be taken if quick action is wanted. There is a great inertia built in by this legal encumberance. These are patent constitutional weaknesses of local government.

Another particular weakness in local government is this procedure of annual budgeting. Estimates for one year are used and therefore the horizon tends to be limited to one year. The politicians are elected every year – in the counties it is every three years – and consequently the political parties have their eyes on a horizon that is never farther away than twelve months. This again is very restrictive.

Authorities that work under two-tier local government face particular problems. In county burghs at least we do have the facility of being able to get officers together, to get chairmen together, to manoeuvre people into a position where there is some form of leadership, some form of dominant pressure within the council. Where a decision requires the good will and cooperation and / or possibly the discipline exercised as between two tiers of government who may be opposed in terms of politics or who may not agree with each other, the position can become quite impossible. Each stands on its own individual powers and you cannot enforce the degree of cooperation as you can with a single-tier authority.

The time span of procedures in local government is attenuated by virtue of the legal processes that one has to go through on things like Compulsory Purchase Orders, Comprehensive Development Areas and other schemes of action where so many rights of objection are available to interested parties. The periods of notice are long, the time one has to wait for enquiries (and the even longer time that one has to wait for the results of enquiries) is such that the lead time on any major development has to be reckoned in terms of at least a quin-quennium. On really major redevelopment schemes like those we are trying to do in the city of Newcastle you have to think in terms of generations before we are going to be able to finish some plans we want to achieve.

There are a number of problems that are associated with the motivations of elected representatives – human problems. There are some elected representatives who feel very much that they are elected by their own particular ward or their own particular constituency and they tend to act for that ward rather than for the benefit of the city as a whole. This varies of course very much from member to member. Some members also have very high-powered hobby-horses; for example, the member who is hoping to get a library. This can be a hobby-horse which he or she will ride almost without regard to any other thing that the council might want to do or which the council should be doing.

The relevance of boundaries needs very little explanation to anybody in this realm. When I tell you that there are nineteen local authorities on Tyneside, any one of which could be passed through in about two or three minutes – you will realize what a hopeless task it is trying to do any planning in any one of them. The job is irrelevant and meaningless and in planning the city of Newcastle-upon-Tyne we have to bear in mind the whole time the fact that this is really the city centre of Tyneside. But it is one thing to bear this in mind; it is another thing to prepare realistic plans to implement them when one remembers that a city centre by itself suffers a tremendous financial burden. There are many services which you have to provide which are essentially regional services, but for which the cost falls inevitably on the rate-payers who live within this completely irrelevant adminis-trative boundary. It may have been highly relevant in 1882 or when the original lines were drawn. It certainly is not relevant in the day of the motor car when Newcastle just virtually sucks in people in the morning and blows them out again in the evening and the whole of Tyneside functions effectively as a single city in terms of commercial and industrial activity, in terms of shopping and leisure.

It is quite impossible to get local authorities to give up their independence and to combine voluntarily. It is very difficult to get any combined voluntary action between local authorities unless the need is so clear that it cannot possibly be gainsaid. We have for instance managed to get a very fine airport in the area by voluntary cooperation. We have managed to float a joint sewerage scheme. This is a formal statutory scheme which will have the right to precept on the local authority. This is fine, but again it militates against achieving the totality of the local government function. Already local government has lost its hospitals, its utilities; it does not carry out the full range of social services, many of which are carried out by the Ministry of Social Insurance. If the local authority keeps having to abandon some of its functions in order to hand them over to an ad hoc committee or an ad hoc board, which has the right to precept on that authority, the result is to effectively disenfranchise the electors of a district from expressing their option for that particular service. Even these services will only be provided, necessary though they are, when the need is outstandingly clear. It has for example been a most difficult job to get a project floated for doing a transportation survey of Tyneside.

It is not possible to reorganize boundaries very easily by the formal process. We have gone through many enquiries on Tyneside from the 1930s onwards. I participated in the last one myself and the idea of a city of Tyneside was killed again. I think that even when we get the report of the Royal Commission on Local Government it will be a difficult thing for the Government to reform local government by legislation. It is not going to be very popular and I should not think this government will regard it as high in its priorities.

There is only one real valid reason for needing a larger local authority. All the arguments about economies of scale are not really the issue. The issue is that Tyneside can be planned as a whole, and this is the big thing that one has to look at. It is the big thing that I hope the Royal Commission is looking at when it is thinking in terms of how big areas of local government, regional government, whatever have you, will be. You have got to look at the relevance of the life of the area, where it all goes on together, interchanges and intertwines. If you could fasten a 100 watt bulb to the head of everybody who was moving around in the area, as it were, and look down, you see a fuzzy pattern of light moving about from time to time. If you could take a film of this then speed it up a thousand times this would develop into a blurr. You could draw a fairly well defined line around that blurr; that would be the right line for the boundary of a single unified local government organization for that area as a whole.

I am quite sure that if Tyneside had had a single unified Government in the late twenties and thirties there would not have been anything near the tragedies and the heart-aches there were then. It would have been powerful enough to get the ear of government. Jarrow, Wallsend and Newcastle by themselves were too small. A fragmented effort just does not work and at the moment there is no one looking at the problems of Tyneside, no one looking at the housing of Tyneside, no one looking at the commercial, the industrial, the economic problems of Tyneside. It is nobody's responsibility. Although Newcastle tries to look at these problems, it is really only doing it 'en passant' because it firstly has to concentrate on its own problems which are intractable enough.

When I came into local government my first reaction to party politics was that this was a great waste of time; if we could get rid of some of this acrimony of party politics and get down to really serious business like discussions and decisions, this would be very good for local government. I am afraid I was soon compelled to take quite a different view of this. It becomes increasingly apparent to anybody working in the heart of local government that party politics are the thing which really make for a virile local government organization.

There is great value in a well organized and dangerous opposition. The opposition forces the party in power to cohere, act, to take decisions to go ahead; the opposition criticizes, it makes sure that decisions are well thought out. I have changed my view quite categorically over the last three years and I fully endorse the value of strong party politics provided there is a good opposition, which is potentially capable of coming into power. (I have had no experience where a party is so dominant that it is never in any danger of losing power. I cannot comment on that.) The majority party is the one that counts in local government – the minority party might as well not be there as far as the actual decision making is concerned.

The majority party however is always in a difficult position as regards its own internal organization. There are rivalries, there are jealousies, there are people seeking after power or privilege or to be in a position where they appear to have gifts of things like commissions, contracts and so on; sometimes even when they may not. They like to appear before the other people in the party as being powerful leaders. These are very human reactions and they play a large part in the way the power is eventually distributed. You do not find much struggle for leadership when a party is in opposition, but when the party is in power and has a gift of power then the leadership disputes increase considerably.

One problem of course is that you are dealing with large numbers –

probably about forty or fifty people – in a party among whom there may be a sort of common political philosophy but no basic loyalty. These people are giving their own time in a voluntary capacity, each is an independent individual, not bound by any constraint or convention to go along with his colleagues. The art of leadership in these circumstances is a very subtle one. I have great admiration for successful political leaders. I think they are very courageous men by and large. It is always difficult to keep a party happy because communication with it is difficult. You cannot let all the people in the ruling party know all that is going on all the time in the sense that they feel they are participating.

If you let them get to the point of feeling that they seldom do participate then you get rumblings and dissentions, and people are not willing to cooperate when the leadership needs cooperation very badly. This is again one of the difficult problems of having so many people without the common tie of having to be responsible jointly for a complex of decisions. It is quite different in industry and commerce, when money is the common tie. Money is a very good tie; it is highly measurable, highly common, highly specific and there is no ambiguity about it.

The exercise of party discipline is something which takes a bit of organizing. The danger is that individual decisions are taken by committees in good faith on fairly logical grounds which in total might be either contradictory or against the basic philosophy of the party that is in control. This may be quite unknown to the committee that is actually taking the decision and is something which officers have to pay a lot of attention to sorting out and which present quite a problem.

Newcastle is setting up a management board – not the Management Board which Maude recommended but the Management Board that Sir Andrew Wheatley came out with in his minority report to Maude. This is very necessary because the policy of the Council as implemented by decisions taken in a whole lot of committees needs to be coherent; the policy should fit together in terms of its social objectives, in terms of the resources which you can afford to deploy on it, in terms of its programming. Many of these things involve major decisions which are political rather than officer inspired decisions. Decisions, for instance, as to whether the authority shall build a housing estate in this area or whether you shall allow a private builder to build a private housing estate in the area. This is the sort of thing which I refer to as basically a political decision. A planner certainly advises that they need to have six hundred houses in that area and he can show them perfectly good reasons why irrespective of which party is in power, one party will want to build a housing estate them-

selves and another will put forward a good case for letting it to a builder
to build a private estate. The Management Board which we are going
to set up will contain members of the majority party only. There is no
room for political argument on a management board. All the meetings
will be in private because if you are trailing your coat and you are
saying something which is slightly off-beat or apparently nonsensical
in order to crystallize the feeling of the meeting, you do not want to
find these statements leering at you over the marmalade pot next
morning in the local press.

Most local authorities of course, have some form of advisory or
policy committee. Local government tends to be unsympathetic to
the idea of boss committees. No committee likes to feel that there is
somebody going to tell it what to do even though it is quite clear to
anybody with any experience of organization at all that you have got
to have a Chief among the Indians. The fundamental belief of many
committee members is that it has got to be all Indians and no chiefs
and this idea of 'democracy' dies very hard. There is a built-in basic
resistance to leadership in local government; this applies at political
level as well as at officer level. Throughout local government, as soon
as you find a strong personality emerging, you find that he is very
hotly contested by other people who feel they ought to be the leader
(and this will particularly apply to the political leaders). The ultra-
democrats feel that there ought to be nobody leading at all and that
the Council ought to be moving ahead in a democratic task without
any leadership.

A councillor must look at things from quite a different view from an
official. He attaches considerable importance, of course, to his public
stance. It is not sufficient that he should take the right decision –
he must be seen to take the right decisions, and he must be seen to be
brilliant at having taken the right decision. His ability to argue in
Council and make a good case comes very high on the list of qualifica-
tions which are required of a political leader. He can possibly be
manoeuvred into the position of taking the right decisions by his
colleagues and the officer corps but it is important that someone
should demonstrate publicly that he and his particular party or his
particular committee has in fact taken these decisions and can justify
them well in public. He must have the ability to impress, particularly
the fourth estate.

Now a word on the formation of policy. Everybody talks about
policy in local government and I often wonder what it means. When,
for the terms of reference of the Management Board which we are
about to set up, I was defining the issues that the Management Board
would take unto itself, I obviously included such things as the approval

of the development plans, the social plan, the leisure plan and any other statutory or non-statutory plans which have a major effect of the life of the city, including the fixing of the rates. But also I was careful to stipulate the obligation on the Chairman of Committees and on the Chief Officers of the Corporation, to bring into the Management Board right in the first instance, any matters of policy. Policy is defined here in terms of matters which are important in themselves, or which have high public visibility even though they are not particularly important. If a member is ever caught taking £5 for voting a certain way it may be relatively unimportant in cash terms, but it would nevertheless be a matter of tremendously high visibility and this is the sort of thing that one would have to discuss at top level.

Some things in local government by their very nature have a very high public visibility content, even though they are relatively unimportant in themselves. Any decision that is likely to involve the council in public criticism, should appear before the management committee. This is important because the council is to all intents and purposes, in a decision-taking capacity, the majority party as far as decision-taking is concerned and one has to have regard to the continued life of the majority party. This, of course, will be very much the interest of the management board. If this sounds like you have an organization and an establishment which is dedicated to the preservation of the majority party for the time being, this is so. These are the facts of life irrespective of whether it is democratic in theory or whether in theory the establishment should be neutral. The facts of life are that the establishment is there to serve what is *effectively* the major political job. When a party goes into opposition its members do not seem to play much role nor to have much contact with the officers at all. They seem to retire into a shell and certainly do not exploit their position as members. They tend not to find out the facts of what is happening nor to exercise their right to any information that exists in the council; this latter may take the form for example of a council document which helps them investigate the particular circumstances they need to look at in exercising their role as a councillor.

It is interesting to look at the impact on members, of the time that they are required to spend on council business. When I went to Newcastle both parties complained bitterly about the fact that we had so many committee meetings, that it took them so long to make decisions and that they had to spend so much time every week on local affairs. Last year we reformed the committee structure and changed their way of operating so that things went through fewer committees, so that the decisions were channelled more directly through council. The work load on members was reduced by 70 per cent – which was a fair start. This change of committee structure coincided with a change of political power and therefore the decrease in work was not a straight 70 per cent across the board. The minority party of course has a smaller representation on committees even though, in total, it was almost numerically equal to the majority party. The work load on what was the minority party but what is now the majority party fell therefore only by about 40 per cent but the work load on what was the majority party and is now the minority party,* fell by something like 80–90 per cent and this raised a chorus of complaint – genuine, sincere complaint – that members in the minority party do not feel that they are playing a significant part as local representatives. This is something that I do not know the answer to; it is a very genuine complaint and is part of the penalty of streamlining your organiza-tion.

It is interesting too, to compare availability of time as between the two parties. By and large the socialist party like to have their meetings during the day and they seem to have plenty of time to attend them. They have plenty of time because most of them are employed in comparatively humble walks of life and they have no problem about getting time off for local government duties. The unions back this proposition and no self-respecting employer can refuse time off to someone who is not a key man. It does not present him with any major difficulty and of course members get reimbursed for the time they spend on formal council business. Many of the leading members of the socialist party were pretty well full-time at the civic centre. The opposition members were rather unkind about this and I have heard it suggested that some of them had jobs which they do not really enjoy and preferred to spend their time in committee. There may be some-thing in this. There were also a fair number of what is called the weaker sex (but which does not always turn out that way in local government), who are usually widows, whose whole life was dedi-cated to local government and who attended the civic centre most of the day. This was the general picture.

Now we have the conservative party in power, professional men, executives, directors of business, senior staff in businesses, young men coming up the promotion ladder in their own firms, assistant bank managers, men of this sort who find it very difficult to get – or take – time off. First of all their employers, their senior partners, their managing directors or their chairmen do not like it. They are key men and their absence affects their work. They get ribbed about 'Are you actually coming into work next week at all?' They do not get

* The people who used to have ten members on each of thirty-seven committees now only have about four members on eight committees.

compensated for any time they spend on council business. Attendance at council is definitely impairing their own personal careers – there is no doubt about that. A chap who is on the way up is working hard and dedicated entirely to his firm. He cannot afford the distraction of local government. Employers know this and these employees therefore tend to get passed over when promotions or new jobs are under consideration. Some of the members, even chairmen of committees, let it be known that they do not wish to be contacted at work – they do not wish their employer even to be aware of their local government activities. Consequently, where there was pressure previously for members to spend a tremendous amount of their time on council affairs, there is now pressure for them to spend as little time as possible. Our meetings now start at 4 o'clock in the afternoon. This was a severe shock to the establishment – particularly the officers – because they now find that they spend all day in their offices running their departments instead of in committee. It is frustrating and inefficient to be full-time during the day with committee members and committees and then to desperately try and catch up with thinking and administrative work in the evening, as it is to rush on through the work in the morning before the committee has got started.

Now a word on the value or otherwise of publicity. The press make an awful fuss about whether committees or council meetings are open to them. This is rather naive because any real discussion that takes place of course on really difficult and thorny subjects has to take place in private for reasons that I have already explained. The press are fairly responsible in Newcastle; they take a sensible view of things and I do not think they deliberately try and provoke difficulties. But, although we have our committee meetings open to the press, you can see when you are actually sitting in committee how many arguments cannot be determined beforehand. They have to be determined in committee. You can see that it is very inhibiting to have the press there. Officers are most unwilling to stick their necks out lest they are rebuked and reported, or lest something they are saying is represented in a way which will the next day in the papers make them look as though they are advocating something which is not good for the city. These sorts of things can happen. I suffered from this recently for instance where I was presenting a report on what we need to do to maintain our housing programme at the very high rate at which it is currently running. One of the things that I said was that we would have to exercise a harsher discipline on tenants who hung on in a clearance area and tried to blackmail us into giving them precisely what they wanted, in preference to top priority cases for that particular type of accommodation. The next morning – I might have guessed it – large headlines saying that I was advocating harsh treatment for council house tenants. The newspapers and radio can only present encapsulated ideas. They have to try and reduce everything to half a dozen words or four inches of newsprint and of course I suppose that they have to have an eye for the thing that will attract attention. The ordinary good common sense decisions do not attract any attention. It is only the things which are bad, scandalous, vulgar or salacious that do receive publicity. I do not think the press is necessarily the right medium for obtaining public participation in local affairs. It is commercially orientated rather than socially orientated and although the lads who write the news are good, honest reporters, they are not always gifted with the ability to present the thing objectively.

I turn now to the officer body. This will probably be more about Newcastle than about other local authorities because I have not had an awful lot of opportunity to observe the way other local authorities work – although I do believe that in Newcastle we have an exceptionally good officer team. I base this not solely on my own evaluation but on that of independent professional people who are required to negotiate with them and who have no real interest in being involved in this evaluation. I am not the boss of all the officers. They are as independent now as they ever were.

I have not tried to change this at Newcastle because I do not believe that leadership is something which you obtain or exercise by having words written on a piece of paper. You get leadership only one way and that is by leading which is a very personal thing and depends very much on the relations which you have with your colleagues. Whether I have had any success at this or not is not the issue in point. I think this is the way local government will best be advised to look for its leaders among its officer corps – not to try and put people into a position of leadership by writing on paper, but to try to appoint to potential positions of leadership, such as to the one I have been appointed, people who can exercise leadership simply by leading. Officers do not like to feel that they are subordinate to anyone. There is a long, long tradition of this that will not die easily in local government. There is no tradition of city managerships such as has grown up in the United States and I do not think the professional institutions of the surveyors, engineers, planners, architects, treasurers and others are about to abdicate in favour of any other particular profession; nor do I think they are about to concur in any legalized form of making their members subordinate to any other particular profession. I do not see any practical difficulty in doing this. I believe it is working in Newcastle.

A problem in the economics of local government is the fact that in business as in local government you can identify the costs and resources you have to use. What you cannot identify in local government, in any government, is the effectiveness. You have a measure of revenue in business and you can take away your cost from your revenue to find out what your profit is; that is a good measure of effectiveness because that is what you are in business for. In local government you cannot add the good you are doing in your health service, the good that you are doing in your housing service, the good that you are doing in renewing the city centre and come out with a sum total. This means that you are constantly faced with a much bigger spectrum of value judgements than you are faced with in business. It is however a question of degree. It is not that you are faced with these things in government and that you are not faced with them in business you are faced with them in business too. When you are faced with judging how effective an advertisement is going to be, or how far you should develop your quality control procedures, you are faced with a value judgement. But in local government you have even more value judgements and it is probably just as well that you do have a fair amount of time in the hands of the people who must eventually decide these value judgements. It is probably appropriate that you should have more people who are the top management (the councillors) in local government, than one would normally expect in business life.

It worries me that there is no way of getting an objective review of how effective local authorities are. I have often played around with ideas about having something like a select committee on estimates – not so much concerned however with the resources which are applied, but with the effectiveness with which they are used. I do not know to what extent it may sometime or other become possible to have another auditor, if we can use that expression, who reports in terms of effectiveness rather than in terms of cost in the same way that an auditor in commercial life audits the effectiveness of the business. He calculates your effectiveness in terms of profit and that is a pretty good commentary on how effective you have been in your business.

If we could have this sort of thing in government, this would be fine but you can see the obvious political pressures and problems that would arise from this sort of review.

The last thing I want to comment on is the calibre of membership of local authorities. As far as I can discern, the calibre of intelligence, drive, integrity and initiative of individuals in local government is pretty well the same as for the population at large. I have no evidence of this except of my own eyes and my acquaintanceships with members of local government in many authorities. I do not think they are any better or any worse than the population at large. This means that if you have a council of about eighty people with say fifty of those in the majority party, there are half a dozen people of high calibre who have got sufficient time to devote to the affairs of the council and they are effectively going to run the affairs of the city. My own ideas as to the number of members of a local authority would be quite different from the figures of eighty that you have for a city like Newcastle which has a quarter of a million population. I should have thought that about seven elected members would be ample. But to do this of course one would need to formalize the delegation of much of the work to the officers and usually this is not legally possible. There are as many regulations that determine specific matters which have to be brought to council. If you are asking council members to take a decision you are bound to explain the facts to them. This absorbs a good deal of time and effort. Not only do the usual management actions of considering and identifying the best courses of action have to be undertaken, they then have to be sold over again to the council. This state of affairs will have to be put right eventually and I think officials will have to learn to take the responsibilities for which they are quite amply paid. The rates of pay in local government are I think quite fair, and it may be argued that officials largely have to bear the responsibility for taking the decisions in as much as their recommendations are so largely accepted by councils. It is one thing to take decisions when somebody else is bearing the ultimate responsibility. It is however quite a different thing to take decisions when you are at the end of the line and you are personally responsible and accountable for them. When reforms do come so that officers are seen to be personally responsible for decision-taking in local government, they will take harder and longer looks at the decisions that they do take and this will be very good for the business of local government. It will make them a lot more critical and a lot more meticulous about their decision taking.

Disscusion

D. LYDDON

I think that the two talks could be linked together by considering that Dr Sharpe was dealing with the setting out of strategies, and Mr Harris was concerned with the reaching of tactical decisions for the actual implementation of values. If one says that this idea of strategy is meaningful at the National and Regional Sub-regional scale, then it is not a matter of making a plan in the sense of something finite and discrete like a building. What one is really concerned with is the planning process as a continuous operation. If perhaps the national economic plan had been put forward in terms of strategy it would have been more acceptable and could have been reviewed in those terms.

On this question of 'assumptions and hunches', I think they should be questioned because this means that they can be improved at the next stage of the continuous process of reviewing strategy. I also think it is meaningful to analyse the past and possible future patterns of 'Urban Forms'. However the danger exists of trying to see a visual coherence in terms of diagrams which may be appropriate to a physical pattern but does not necessarily mean that there is a social coherence. These elements should help towards a strategy, which is the setting out of long term possibilities and short term opportunities. Within this, there is the tactical side, which implies picking up the short term opportunities and translating them into action on the lines that Mr Harris put forward.

My basic question to Dr Sharpe, is to ask if he feels that the integrating of economic planning and land use planning could be achieved by thinking and setting out more in terms of strategy than by the greater definition of a Land Use Plan? And would Mr Harris feel that his own implementation of the tactics of putting across the ideas would be easier if it had a background of strategy laid out?

L. J. Sharpe. There are simply two things. First you define sociogeographic coherence. Assuming you can, is it possible to transfer this into meaningful boundaries? How far can you go on the socio-geographic side in discovering meaningful boundaries for other sorts of activities, such as, economic planning or the whole range of local services? I have some strong doubts about this because I do not think there is a socio-geographic order. I think one must ask in the first place what sort of level one is concerned with, and then one can find various evidence to either refute or support this, but you have to have some notion of order. You can define an actual cell which is on the scale of a neighbourhood or a village, and you can define, an actual cell which is on the level of a cultural region. In the middle you can find other natural cells. But I do not think there are any clear divisions. This may be a function of the data, in that the activity or the process is there but we only have very, very small areas where we have a straight flow of events.

I did not mention in the paper that in Britain we are expecting

EC M

government to take on an executant operational role; the whole nature of central administration in Britain is against it however. The tradition of the administrative class in Britain is essentially one of governing, controlling and inspecting – of setting the limits. The problem that faces the British government over the next ten to fifteen years, put in very dramatic terms, is the extent to which central government actually transforms itself and becomes an operational authority. Experience suggests that the central government is not very well attuned to this kind of activity.

D. Lyddon. Do you think central government or reorganized local government at regional levels could operate effectively in terms of a 'strategy', which would be their executive document?

L.J. Sharpe. I do not think that you can have an effective regional body unless it has an executive role. But this seems to me a highly doubtful proposition, as somebody has got to do the actual land use planning and as they will want to deal with Whitehall which is where the power will lie.

W. F. Harris. I do not see why development strategy should not proceed by dialogue right from national level to parish level and back again up and down. This is a perfectly normal basis of developing commercial and industrial strategy and I do not see why given a few years, putting it into shape and practising it, we should not develop it with a reformed local government. At the moment, of course, with the Ministry – say the Ministry of Housing and Local Government – exercising the span of control over 1,500 local authorities, you cannot do it as there is no hierarchy of governmental agencies and the executive roles being clearly defined. I am quite sure it could happen.

It is a great pity to see the National Plan disappear, even although it was a 'national hope' not a National Plan. A plan is only feasible when it has been demonstrated and agreed by those who have to carry it out. This is the first thing; we have to develop a National Plan in which all the people who have to carry it out do, in fact, concur and agree; until we get that, we shall not have a strategy that is viable.

J. CORNFORD

What I am interested in is the tactical consideration of what one might call the recruitment of the people who are actually going to run whatever type of reformed local government one gets. Even if we could attract far better people at the officer level there is the problem of councillors.

When Mr Harris was talking about committee decision and the

time given by various councillors, the thing that strikes me most about the relationship between the commitment of councillors is that they are not there because they are interested in policy.

One of the problems I think about limiting the number of councillors to seven or eight is that there is absolutely no guarantee that the parties would deliver you the seven or eight who understand the business or who are interested in it. If you have eighty to choose from there is some chance of you getting them; if you have eight I would not guarantee that the people who get to the top in the party system are the people who would be good doing the business. I think this is a very real difficulty. One thinks that the people with the best kind of training who would be most able people, are also the least likely to want to spend the time on that kind of work. In some councils one is struck by the fact that, the younger and more able members of the council are clearly going to last a very short time. The ones who remain are those people who make a career out of council work maybe because they do not need to spend much time running their own family business or they work in a nationalized industry which will give them any time off and so forth. These people who get committed to council work will stay long enough to achieve a position of leadership. This is not actually very closely connected with ability and although I agree with you that there may be very important political skills involved in survival for that long, the survival value of these members may not translate very well into good effective policy making.

W.F. Harris. I do not know how we are going to recruit better councillors. More is not the answer. I think if you got down to far smaller numbers, the party machines would have to produce their best men. They would have to produce the men who are going to do the party credit.

If you have a small number like seven or ten or twenty, the party machines will distill their best because this is a survival mechanism. The party will not survive if it puts inefficient people in power, and they make bad decisions. They will put their best people in power and if the numbers are small enough they could find those with the required degree of competence.

I am glad Professor Cornford raised this question of motivation of councillors because I went to some pains to see every member of Newcastle City council in the first year I was there. I have seen everyone who has come into the council since and one of the things I have asked every one of them is, Why are you in the council? Professor Cornford in quite right, there is nobody who has said that the reason is because they enjoy making policy decisions, or they enjoy hard decision taking, or management or anything like that. They vary from the woman who said that she was in local government because she wanted to do something for the generation that had gone before her, the old people – that was her sole motivation for being in local government. I spoke to a newly elected conservative councillor the other day, a young fellow, and he said that he had come in because it seems a natural progression from the Young Conservatives. I then asked him why he was in the Young Conservatives and he answered that they were a 'jolly nice crowd'. That was his motivation for coming into local government, and they are as varied as this. People do not know what goes on in local government until they get into it and they have been in for several years, got a really good feel of it, probably been Chairman of a Committee, got a taste for power and a taste for decision taking; then this knowledge begins to emerge although it takes some little while to come through. It seems to emerge probably more quickly from the socialist side because they have a number of fairly well established institutions like trade unions where you can get this sort of experience. Cooperative Societies are another thing where you can get this sort of experience coming through, and they take to council work fairly readily. This probably gives them a foretaste of what is going to happen. But they have no more idea why they come into the council than most of us have when we take up our next job.

JOHN ERICKSON
I would like to ask Mr Sharpe the significance of this word 'Regional'. This is not a question, this is an observation.

I thought that Mr Sharpe very admirably distinguished two types of regionalism when he pointed out the difference in administrative techniques and objectives. I have myself noted down the fact that it seemed to be in a sense three.

First of all there is this kind of technological impulse of transformation which is part of the centralist regionalism. Secondly there seems to be a functional regionalism which is a combination of administrative techniques and some kind of economic objectives. There seems to me to be a third type of regionalism which is derived basically from a sort of cultural nationalism. As to the sort of politics of setting up a region, the thing of which one has to take account of ultimately is this semi-disguised cultural nationalism.

I am grateful to Mr Lyddon for bringing up the words strategy and tactics. The Russians do not believe in a simple distinction between 'Strategy' and 'Tactics'. They have a 'Grand Strategy', 'Operating Art', and 'Tactics'. It seems to me that what is wrong in regionalism is that there is no 'Operating Art'. Operating art consists of things like institutional arrangements – it is this middle bit between strategy and tactics.

L. J. Sharpe. I accept clearly Professor Erickson's point about cultural nationalism being really a third factor – but it is of a different order to the other things because it is not related to systematic assessment of problems.

It is not also just a simple question of centralization; local government in some form exercising a degree of local autonomy is a necessity of life in a complex modern democracy. So in a sense this really leaves your first definition aside. It means it is not just a question of centralism, it is a question of how you tackle the functional requirements, for a whole range of services. Some may be appropriately done through what we call local government and others not.

I entirely agree with Mr Harris. If you are selling something, you need some crude criterion of performance, If you are not, you are in the extraordinary position like the Hospital Service where all the money comes from one central source and you have a vast bureaucratic structure. You are not responsive to anything in the sense that you do not have respresentative members pushing you along as it were, vaguely reflecting needs. You are in a sort of limbo, you have neither autonomy nor do you have any primary propelling interest.

P. E. A. Johnson-Marshall. In Mr Sharpe's background study of the growth of regionalism and the attempts to achieve it, a case could be made for including a reference to the Barlow Report because this set the fundamental framework of land use combined with the economic assessment of industrial and population distributions. I think the significant thing was that when the Ministry of Town and Country Planning was set up, they cut away any economic duties which were left in the Board of Trade. We still need a combined Economic and Land Use Plan.

I would like to put, if I may, an idea that we might have an operation which interacts between the top and the bottom. I think there is a gap in thinking here; people have been muddling up levels and I think there is a Provincial level which has not been discussed. I would suggest that there might well be a case for the British Isles to be considered in terms of Provinces because I think there is quite a different operational task between the nature of a Province and the duty of a Region; this could well be examined rather carefully as to whether we should not have a Provincial Organization. This level would wipe out the County which seems to me a ridiculous hangover.

I would strongly agree that the Ministry of Housing and Local Government is also a kind of hangover.

Mr Harris has opened up a broader concept of the interaction between large organizational teams. I would like to see this looked at, in terms of central government and even perhaps universities. I would also like to feel there was a good deal more of this interaction that he has described, if local government is to become a desirable place for human beings to work in. To achieve this, I think it is really vital to attract top quality technical people in the planning sphere.

W.F. Harris. One of the problems about local government is its career structure. You can very seldom provide a whole career structure within any one particular local authority. The bigger county burghs might be able to do this and in certain cases some of the counties might be able to do it. In some of the very heavily populated areas somebody can live within range where he can probably switch jobs from one local authority to another half a dozen times without shifting his house. If however, somebody has reached a position where he can only be employed by a local authority of 250,000 and he is currently employed by Newcastle, then his next step is to go to another local authority somewhere else for a next step up the ladder because there is not a likely vacancy going to occur within his lifetime in Newcastle. He has therefore to pick up his house and go, because there is not another local authority that size anywhere around. This is a very considerable problem in local government. I do not think that in terms of its technical officers – by technical I mean engineers, architects, planners, doctors, accountants, lawyers, etc. – I do not think that I observe much differences between the worst in local government and the worst in industry. By and large the basic calibre of the staff is similar as between the two. In each field you get the dedicated few who are there all hours and utterly dedicated to the job, throwing themselves into it with almost a complete disregard for the money they get. And you get the others who watch the clock and as soon as it gets round to twenty-nine minutes past four they are off towards the hat stand. You get this in both fields. I certainly think local government provides excellent opportunities and probably wider horizons for many technical people than many jobs in industry or even in private practice. This is certainly true in the fields of architecture and law and things like this, but I think you cannot do anything but good by swapping experiences. One of our youngsters, is just going into private practice for two or three years and he is doing it with our blessing on the assurance he will be welcome to come back. We think he will be a better man in the end and I am sure this is just plain good common sense management. You know that he will have had more experience, that he will have learned something outside and that he will not be completely inbred within the organisation.

L. J. Sharpe. I think Professor Johnson-Marshall's provincial idea is very interesting and one could conceive of going for a provincial level rather than a city regional level on the grounds that the problem is really to fit the round peg functions into the square hole of areas. Of course, you would always fit round pegs in square holes providing the square hole is big enough, and on the assumption that you cannot predict the future, and this is what we all face, if you make your square holes big enough you can possibly meet what seems to be a general tendency to have a rather wider area of operation rather than a narrower one in the field of planning and economic services.

Part Five . Transport

Urban Transportation Planning
R. *White, Professor of Civil Engineering*
University of Newcastle upon Tyne

Discussion :
P.K. *McIlroy*
Messrs Freeman Fox, Wilbur Smith and Associates, Edinburgh
W.D.C. *Wright, Lecturer,*
Department of Economics, University of Edinburgh

Urban Transportation Planning

R. WHITE

R. WHITE

TRANSPORTATION PLANNING IN RETROSPECT

The planning of urban highway networks before the Second World War was generally based on conformity with an idealized geometric plan. Although regular counts of volume of traffic were made at points on British highways since the beginning of the century, the information obtained was used primarily for design of elements of networks, for example, intersections, and little was known of the pattern of movement.

Most literature on highway and town planning classified highway networks in urban areas into groups, 'grid-iron', 'radial' or 'linear'. It was sometimes claimed that these patterns were apparent from a study of plans of existing cities. If reports of modern traffic studies are examined or if plans of cities prepared by motoring organizations to show through routes and congested routes are studied, it will be found difficult to classify highway patterns if usage is considered instead of purely geometric pattern.

By the 1920s it was recognized that the adoption of idealized patterns took little quantitative account of demand for movement in relation to the motive or purpose, and origin-and-destination surveys began. There also began attempts to relate traffic movements to parameters of land-use. When projections for the future were made, the simple process of expanding existing volumes by the known annual rate of growth was adopted. The Ministry of Transport recommendation (1946) was that provision should be made for a volume double that prevailing before the war. Taking the country as a whole, this figure was attained in 1955 and double the 1955 figure was attained in 1964. In the United States a forecast was made in 1934 that there would be 34 million vehicles in 1940 and 42 million in 1960. The forecast for 1940 was correct (within reasonable limits) but the figure forecast for 1960 was attained in 1948 and the 1960 figure was actually 74 million.

These early estimates did not take account of the rise in the standard of living, the movement to the suburbs, the growth in two-car families, and the accelerated decline in public transport associated with increased car ownership and causing in turn increased car usage.

Estimation of future traffic must therefore take account of changes in economic and social condition and, when a detailed network in a given town is being studied, there must be regard to the changes likely to be made in the disposition of the various uses of land.

Techniques currently in use attempt to relate travel to social and economic factors associated with land-use and a summary of these techniques follows.

CURRENT TECHNIQUES OF TRANSPORTATION PLANNING

For the forecasting of future travel patterns various models are used which attempt to express in quantitative forms the relations between movements and the social and economic activities which create movement. There are four main groups of such models although there are many modifications to be found in each group.

The first group is based on the statement that traffic between two areas (or zones) is a function of the land use activity in each zone and of the resistance to travel between them. In its simplest form this may be expressed:

$$T_{i-j} = K\frac{P_i P_j}{d_{i-j}^b}$$

where T_{i-j} = trips between zone i and zone j

P_i = a parameter for zone i such as population, ratable value, area of shops, number of workplaces, depending on the type of trip being studied

P_j = a similar parameter for zone j

d_{i-j} = a measure of the resistance to travel between zones i and j depending on time, distance, or cost of travel

K = a constant

b = an exponent

From the similarity between this formula and the formula for the Law of Gravity, this model is sometimes called the 'Gravity Model'.

When dealing with the urban problem, the engineer is generally concerned with a complex of zones and its concomitant network and the model is more usefully expressed in the form:

$$T_{i-j} = P_i \ \frac{\dfrac{A_j}{d_{i-j}^b}}{\dfrac{A_i}{d_{i-i}^b} + \dfrac{A_j}{d_{i-j}^b} + \ldots + \dfrac{A_n}{d_{i-n}^b}}$$

where P_i = total trips produced by zone i
A_j = total attraction of zone j
T_{i-j}, d_{i-j} and b as before

It has been found that this model does not give very good results for very short or very long distances between zones. This is not surprising as small differences of distance or journey time are unlikely to affect travel choice and long journeys are likely to have to be undertaken by the traveller for reasons which are relatively independent of distance or time. Models have been derived, therefore, which adapt the formula mathematically to allow for the effect of very short or very long inter-zonal distances.

The second group of models may be described as 'growth factor' methods. This group may be described as follows in symbolic terms:

$$T_{i-j} = G_i t_i \frac{G_j t_{i-j}}{\sum\limits_{x=1}^{n} G_x t_x}$$

where T_{i-j} = future total trips between zones i and j estimated from zone i; $i, j = 1 \dots n$
G_i = growth factor, zone i
t_i = present trip ends in zone i
t_{i-j} = present trips $i-j$ and $j-i$
$\sum\limits_{x=1}^{n} G_x t_x$ = sum of products of all present trips from zone i and growth factor of opposite zones

Consider a simple example of movement between two zones A and B. Let the present trips between the two zones be 10. If for the design year it is estimated that trips from zone A will grow by a factor of 2, then 20 trips will be created from zone A to B. If trips from Zone B are expected to grow by a factor of 3, then 30 trips will be created from Zone B to A. Clearly the two figures should be equal and using the above formula, a reiterative process is used whereby successive growth factors are calculated until each interzonal movement is represented by a single figure and the total from each zone is consistent with the growth factor for the zone.

There are modifications to this method of a technical nature and means are used to overcome the diffculty of a zone which is at present under-developed and for which there is no figure of present traffic.

The third group may be described as the intervening opportunity model. This model assumes that the traveller keeps his journey as short as possible, i.e. fulfils his purpose at first location.

The probability of ending a journey in a selected zone is:

$$(1-p)^V - (1-p)^{V+U}$$

where p = probability of certain type of trip stopping at any randomly selected point

V = number of trip destinations within zone considered lying closer to origin than specific randomly selected point

U = number of zonal trip destinations closer to origin than zone containing selected point

Lastly, some progress has been made in recent years in the application of linear programming methods, that is to say, a pattern of travel in relation to land use is found which minimizes the amount of travel on the assumption that travellers individually minimize cost of travel.

The basic information for use in the above procedures is obtained by field surveys which seek to find out the origin and destination of each trip, the purpose of the trip, the method of travel, the socio-economic group of the traveller. The latter information is associated with land-use information such as rateable value of the home, some of which can be derived from public records without separate field studies. The surveys required are generally.

(*a*) cordon survey (roadside interview), to obtain details of movements in to, out of, and through the study area.

(*b*) home questionnaire survey, to obtain details of travel within the study area, and social and economic data.

(*c*) industrial and commercial employees' survey to determine movements by people from outside the study area not detected by other surveys and to associate movement with type of industry and commerce.

(*d*) public transport survey, to obtain travel details of people not intercepted by the other studies.

(*e*) goods vehicles survey, to obtain details of goods deliveries within the area.

From the information one or more repression equations may be obtained which give the relationship between trips and the land-use, social and economic factors generating such trips. Desire lines of travel, that is the interzonal volumes between zones irrespective of route used are obtained.

The future land-use plan is then examined and the future details of land-use substituted in the regression equations to obtain the future generation of trips in each zone.

In the case of the so-called 'gravity models', the indices to be used are obtained from a calibration of the existing desire line data.

The future travel pattern of desire lines is then calculated using one of the models outlined above.

Having obtained the desire lines of future travel, the trips represented by these desire lines have to be assigned to method of travel, private or public, and if public, whether bus or rail, insofar as choice is likely to exist. In the case of private travel the trips have to be assigned to elements of the proposed road network.

The allocation of trips to modes of transport ('the modal split') may be made at different stages in the process, before trip generation is estimated, or after trip generation and before distribution or after the desire line pattern has been obtained. If carried out at the earlier stages, the assumption is implicit that public transport will not change its nature in future and decisions are tied to the relationships given by trip generation equations derived from present day conditions. If carried out after the desire lines are estimated, some examination is possible of the effect of new and improved forms of travel.

For a given mode of travel it is necessary to assign the movements to elements of the road network as already mentioned, and such assignment is generally made on the assumption that the traveller minimizes journey time, distance or cost or a combination of these factors. Generally, trial assignments with existing desire lines are made to the existing network until volumes are obtained which correspond to the recorded volumes on the roads concerned.

The techniques permit the testing of alternative road networks and alternative distributions of land-uses and also allow a 'feed-back' to the generation stage in the case of models which take accessibility into account in their construction. Physical and economic limitations on the location of highways and similar limitations on the distribution of proposed new land-uses limit the number of alternative schemes which it is necessary to test. This process ought to allow for the reciprocal effect of transportation and the accessibility achieved by transportation systems on the proposed land-use plan but in practice little use seems to be made of this ability as will be discussed later.

The limiting capacity of highways of given geometric character and of intersections between highways must be taken account of in the assignment process, as it may be neither economic nor practical to provide always for assigned volumes on particular routes. The journey times or costs used in the assignment must then be adjusted and the process repeated.

CRITICISM OF TRANSPORTATION PLANNING TECHNIQUES

Leaving aside technical criticism of detailed methods of interest only to practitioners, the general procedure requires to be examined critically to see how far travel patterns may be estimated in relation to the social and economic forces which produce travel. The general statement commonly made is that traffic is a function of land-use. This is obviously true in relation to the home-base of the traveller and while it is true that the destination, e.g. workplace, shop, school, business call is associated directly with its geographic position, the interaction between them will vary according to the restraints placed on the traveller. For example, it was not uncommon in the early part of the century for a shipyard worker on the Clyde to move his home in accordance with the distribution of his trade to new ships being built in different yards. Such mobility is uncommon now, nor is it certain that people would wish their homes to be so mobile. They may prefer to use the improved means of transport, especially personal transport, to gain mobility.

The models in current use have existing restraints on mobility built into them and they express travel quantitatively in terms of land-use and social factors only to the extent that these factors can be measured and the data made available. The parameters in general use are, population, socio-economic group, rateable value of the house, with minor variations such as number in family, number of driving licences in home. Certain parameters may be used for certain journey purposes and others for other purposes. The tendency, therefore, is to consider that the regression equations tell the whole story when in fact other elements are omitted either because they cannot be measured or because they are not yet fully understood. These factors will be mentioned below but in the meantime traffic engineers are well aware of the limitations of their technique and look to the other professions involved to provide the information.

The second aspect of urban travel involved in the prediction models used is the 'modal split' or the determination of which methods of transport people will use. Here again, the engineer has to rely on current data. An example of one aspect of this particular procedure is to estimate the parking spaces likely to be available in the central urban area to estimate the capacity of the highways to match, and to assume that the journeys which cannot be made by car because of parking restraints will be made by public transport. This will be examined more fully later.

The third stage in the process which requires special mention is the 'assignment' procedure. The assumption, as mentioned above, is that the choice of route is based on shortest time, distance or cost. The model is 'calibrated' to existing figures in order to make the assumption fit. The most obvious criticism is that it seems likely in many cases that drivers chose a route which is psychologically apparently quicker than an alternative. The traffic engineer would require anything between 10 and 40 runs timed with a stop-watch and related to steady conditions of volume before he would estimate a journey time between two points with a reasonable degree of reliability and it is quite clear that ordinary drivers make no such systematic determination of journey time.

More will be said on these points below.

In spite of these criticisms, it would appear that the models used have shown a considerable measure of reliability in cases where sufficient time has elapsed to enable an estimate to be verified. This situation has generally been confined to the US A although assignment procedures for short-term periods of time have been checked in this country showing reasonable reliability. This is to be expected as the time is sufficiently short to prevent any major change in driver motive in route selection from developing.

In this country, plans prepared using the techniques mentioned have not been implemented to a stage to enable the techniques to be verified.

If they are verified, there might well be a suspicion that to build a highway system to the plan makes the plan correct as development must conform to the facilities provided, which brings us to the next consideration below.

INTERACTION BETWEEN TRAFFIC AND LAND-USE

Clearly no consideration of urban growth can avoid the study of the impact of travel and modern industrialized and urban society depends on mobility to a degree hitherto unknown. The techniques described above can test land-use dispositions for the optimising of travel just as easily as highway patterns can be tested. There it little evidence that this has been done to any great extent in the recent past.

Generally, in the preparation of transportation and land-use plans little time is available for this process. Usually a preconceived idea of a highway plan has to be justified or the techniques are used to establish traffic volumes for detailed design of features of a network already settled. Similarly, the areas of future development are already defined to a point where major changes would be politically difficult.

There is evidence, in particular from the history of the London Underground, that the construction of travel facilities creates land development though clearly there are limitations to this process. A travel facility cannot of itself create a development but can only enable a potential development to be exploited. How far should urban growth be either stimulated or directed by the positive use of transportation facilities? In other words should the growth of cities of the future be dominated by the need for accessibility and high mobility? This, of course, is the main theme of the Buchanan Report which shows that once the quality of the environment has been defined, the ability to cope with traffic is determined.

Measures can be taken to ensure the limitation of access to a given area at a given level. Such measures may take the form of parking control, road pricing, geometric and capacity control by the road itself, permits and the multitude of other solutions proposed for the solution of the problem of congestion. Two points arise – first, what happens to the frustrated traffic, second, what is the influence at the other end of the journey? Those who propose measures for the solution of the problem of congestion concentrate only on the city and the journey (primarily work, business and shopping journeys) and say little about the origin of the journey.

In so far as traffic prevented from entering city centres by any given measures is free to choose, the object of the journey will be fulfilled elsewhere. This is the situation which gives rise to the suburban shopping centre. Similarly, in some cities, there is a drift of offices to erstwhile dwellings in the inner suburbs converting the one-time graceful townhouses into inconvenient office accommodation while new office tower blocks remain unoccupied.

The second point relates to residential areas primarily. If easy accessibility to the city centre by private transport is denied perhaps choice of residence will be affected. Will people who must travel to the city decide to live within easy reach of public transport and if they do wish to do so will it be possible? Alternatively, will they use personal transport to a point of transfer to public services? 'Park-and-ride' schemes have not been a conspicuous success so far.

These interactions can be studied to a certain extent by current models of transportation planning but there are serious limitations. The present models use generation equations which have as independent variables relatively easily ascertainable quantities. There may be other factors governing travel, some of which may not be easily measurable, especially those relating to motives for travel and motives determining route choice. Even measurable factors may be deceptive; for instance, car-owners who recover all or part of the cost of car-ownership and use from business sources are likely to be affected less by economic considerations than purely private owners. They may also be less affected by deterrent measures such as road pricing or parking charges. When, by acceptable objective standards, it can be shown that for a particular journey, public transport is more efficient, a high proportion of travellers will choose private transport in spite of congestion, cost, loss of time and temper.

The problem of route choice has already been mentioned and real motives in route choice are not fully understood. Some research is needed here by psychologists and sociologists. The simulation studies used by the traffic engineer may serve their purpose but it is unsatisfactory to know how to obtain an answer without knowing the real underlying theory.

Before leaving the question of interaction between traffic and land-use, it must be mentioned that the traffic engineer's techniques are open to the objection that they extrapolate existing trends to the future albeit in a more refined way than the methods referred to earlier. This may be true, but when the traffic engineer seeks from the other professions involved, some estimation of future trends he finds the same process of projecting existing trends.

It is doubtful how far we can ever go beyond this degree of prediction but some attempt has to be made to formulate a policy for urban growth. The procedure of formulating a 'plan' for twenty years and working strictly to such a plan rigidly is now outdated and recognition is now given to planning as a process subject to continual checking and revision with new proposals tested for their interaction with other elements. A continuous process of this sort is now possible with the aid of computers and the updating of data should be simple with modern data processing facilities. The difficulty is that most of the data as collected at present is not in suitable form nor is data associated with areas of land-use in a manner useful for transportation planning purposes.

PLANNING OBJECTIVES AND TRANSPORTATION

The transportation planner must work in the context of an urban planning policy. In this country, planning policy is subject to ultimate control by the people themselves through their elected representatives but the technical process is obviously multi-disciplinary. I am not qualified to discuss urban planning policy or techniques and the following questions in connection with the nature of the future city are those which bear directly on transportation and in particular are, in my view, the concern of the social scientist.

Who is to specify the nature of the city of the future? Many architects and planners have described the 'ideal' city and the ideal conditions for harmonious and happy community life in a modern city but there appears to be no way of knowing what kind of city the public want, still less of knowing whether they are prepared to pay the price of achievement of the ideal. Besides, any ideal includes imponderable qualities to which economic values cannot be ascribed.

It is doubtful if the public appreciate the powerful forces of change which are at work in cities as a result of modern communications and the inherent resistance to change tends to make people accept the state to which they have been conditioned. (In Glasgow, one hears, people complain about the drastic changes involved in the construction of new highways and at the same time complain about the inadequate traffic system.)

Although I have stated the difficulty of ascertaining what kind of city people want, I shall take the risk of begging some of the questions. For instance, it seems to me that most people look for two conflicting requirements, a home in near-country surroundings, and the facilities of a large bustling city centre. From a transportation point of view, this is what was meant earlier when it was pointed out that there are two ends to most urban travel, one with a high density of demand and the other with a low density of demand. This is the inherent problem of public transport from an economic point of view. If we continue to build to low densities in the suburbs then economically self-supporting mass public transport systems are not possible. The question arises whether we should build to higher densities in order to base movement in cities on public transport systems. The social scientist can perhaps tell us whether other qualities of city life would be sacrificed if higher densities are used. It is not even clear that high-speed, high-quality easily accessible and economic public transport can compete with personal transport. Perhaps the answer is to base urban movement on completely new systems which allow quick personal movement by travelling platforms or devices of a similar nature. The trouble with ingenious systems of this kind is that they cannot be built into existing cities during the process of continuous change and redevelopment but must be built almost completely at the outset.

Is the high-density city centre an outmoded concept or will the persistence of the city through all historical change continue? Much work is being done to examine the relation between the size and structure of a city and the amount of movement which can be sustained at stated levels of congestion. For a full discussion of this subject reference should be made to 'Traffic Studies and Urban Congestion' by Professor R. O. Smeed (*Journal of Transport Economics and Policy*, Vol. 11, No. 1, Jan. 1968). Professor Smeed has shown that for certain sizes of town, time spent on travel for the work journey would be less if all commuters travelled by car instead of bus. The reverse is true of large cities. Professor Buchanan also pointed out in *Traffic in Towns* that the ability of a town to deal with the growth of personal transport is related to its size. Two most commonly recurring attitudes are: 'We must not let the motor-car dominate our cities' and 'We must develop public transport and use it as the main means of city transport'. In fact, while these notes were being prepared the Transport Manager of Glasgow Corporation was reported as saying that the day might come when the private car would be banned from parts of the city centre. Such generalizations are inconsistent with the findings of Smeed, Buchanan and others.

It is clear that each town is an individual product of forces relating to the region of which it is the centre. The new dimension of mobility has a reciprocal effect on the town structure without doubt but each case should be examined individually. The transportation planner can play his part but he will depend on the collaboration of the urban planner, the economist and the social scientist in the process.

Discussion

P. K. MCILROY

I want to pick out two main points of criticism of the present state of the planning art. The first is in the technique of an assignment of traffic to road networks and to public transport networks. The method that has been adopted until recently has been to establish the desire to travel from one point to another and to place all traffic on the route that is shortest in time, cost or distance. This has been bothering all concerned with transport for a long time. There are now techniques of assigning to networks not just of the minimum time parts but also to the next shortest time and the next again. A much more sophisticated technique has been developed and is now being used.

Another general point is that it was not obvious a few years ago, that the household is the basic unit for generation of travel. For example, car ownership is one of the three or four factors that are really important in deciding upon travel. Car ownership is very strongly related to household income and the number of people in the household who are actually workers. It has been discovered that you can categorize households in these terms and that each category of household has a characteristic trip making pattern.

Another criticism concerns the lack of appreciation of all inter-relationships including a proper feedback of traffic data into land use. Although we are beginning to overcome this one, I do not think that anybody should claim that we really understand fully what these relationships are or what they mean. I think though that we are able to demonstrate that they exist. I think now that the main thing that has got to be done is to decide what we are going to do with these studies.

One major piece of research which needs undertaking lies in

assessing the real value of time saved in making a journey by one system as opposed to making it by another system. Benefit studies that go with these things are very crude indeed at the moment. I think, for instance, that possibly the most important thing in about twenty years time is not going to be the journey to work which everybody seems to concentrate on. Leisure trips, social recreation trips, are the ones that are going to grow very rapidly. How do you value the time saved on a leisure trip, a man going with his family to a beach for example. If the trip takes five minutes less, is that a social benefit and if it is what is the value of it?

The other very popular thing of course is to talk of the value of the amenity of the environment. If we are going to compare plans for the future in our cities and in our regions, we must begin to put values on noise and visual intrusion and so on. If we were able to evaluate these things properly we could better compare one system against others as we propose to do. What happens to these plans? Governments and local authorities pay very large sums of money for land use transportation studies to be done. The terms of reference are nearly always to study the present situation and to calibrate a model. This model can reproduce the present situation and then preconceived plans of roads or public transport and arrangements of land use, are tested.

There is however a reluctance to make further use of the models and to test alternatives. After the preconceived one has been tested and the imperfections demonstrated it appears to become embarrassing to look for alternatives. It is a great shame after a million pounds is spent in the London traffic survey and transportation study that we ended up by testing only three different road patterns with two fairly similar public transport patterns and one land use pattern. It seems to me that having created a tool of this nature and complexity it could be a wonderful method for testing alternative policy options in land use planning particularly. Is this lack of application because people distrust the method or perhaps do not understand the method that is being used? If this is the case is it the consultants' fault for not explaining themselves more clearly? Alternatively is it that people do not really want to have a fully defined optimum plan? This point was brought out by Mr Sharpe who instinctively felt that government does not want a detailed committed plan.

R. *White*. A lot of these techniques for assignment to shortest time patterns are still nevertheless simulation techniques. They set up certain assumptions, they test them in a real situation as far as can be done. If the thing works then they accept the process although we have really not got right down to the motivation which underlies the traffic decisions. The technique hands over to the computer some sort of reiterative process that comes out with an answer.

In smaller networks particularly, I prefer to do a shortest time path and see what happens; then I formulate certain capacities based on engineering principles and put the thing in again and see what effect this judgement has had on the model. This way it is kept under control right through. To do this with bigger networks is a bit more difficult and there is a tendency to leave the computer to do it, on a sausage machine technique which might have its dangers.

You mentioned the linking of trips to parameters of land use in the category analysis. We have been asked by the Scottish Development Department to use a study that we are doing in East Kilbride at the moment as a case study. We still intend to use our own methods so far as recommendations to the authorities are concerned but also to use the category analysis in parallel for research purposes. One problem confronting us concerns the distribution of trips. Trips begin in the home and you can categorize these in the way you mentioned but their distribution between zones seems to be something that has not been resolved. This is not a new concept. Early publications on traffic estimation start off at the very beginning with statements that the home is the origin of all trips and all movements and it is to the home that we should look for the motivation and mainsprings of movement.

The quantification of time in leisure trips presents a number of problems. Sir William Glandel once described how in Rome on a Sunday in the summer there is a certain train which leaves in the morning – an express train to a resort which has a beach; this is a non-stop express and you pay a surcharge to travel on it. It is followed a few minutes later by the departure of an ordinary train which stops at all the intermediate stations and finishes up something like forty minutes later at this resort. The families in Rome are clamouring at the iron gates with their children and their balloons and their buckets and spades to get on the early train with the surcharge. What are they paying this surcharge for? Forty minutes more on the beach or a better position on the beach. Well, these people were prepared to pay this extra for forty minutes on the beach therefore that is the economic value of that leisure time spent on the beach.

If one looks at the car sleeper services to the continent and finds out how much people are prepared to pay, you can actually identify where the traffic comes from and find out how much extra people are prepared to pay to gain extra holiday on the continent. I think it can be calculated in sufficient cases to give one some kind of measure.

I turn to the point about reluctance to implement transportation plans. I think these transportation plans are forced on many authorities. I could quote two instances in my own experience where there are very good reasons for believing that authorities were told by a government that they must have a transportation plan before their quinquennial review would be looked at. I think a lot of this transport planning is just fashionable because the Americans do it. As I have said earlier there is frequently the attitude that the land use plan is already crystallized and nobody is going to change it in spite of any traffic engineer coming up with fancy plans that he knows they have not the money to implement anyway.

W. D. C. WRIGHT
Transport seems to be one field in urban planning where quantification is developing fairly rapidly, and I will try to restrict my contribution to the identification of some problems which surround this quantification.

I will start with the question of the valuation of time. Professor White was mentioning the people who use the fastest train from Rome. The difficulty is to determine what it is that is being valued. Is it the time spent upon the beach or the lesser discomfort of shorter time travelling or the better position on the beach or some combination of them and/or other factors? We need to be able to distinguish if we are to be able to use this to value the time saved in other activities.

On a more general level it does seem that quantification that has gone on in the past has often been of a fairly descriptive character. I refer here for example, to the use of the gravity model which has been used to describe relationships between traffic flows, between two given points. It has been of some use in terms of urban planning but has not really dealt with the whole problem of why it is that people do make decisions to travel between two areas.

This problem of quantification can be reflected again in the rather dangerous use of regression analysis. I shall demonstrate the biases which can be engendered in regression analysis by an example. The 'percentage of through traffic' has been regressed on 'level of population'. Location is likely to be a factor interacting with percentage of through traffic and level of population. So that if you really are to understand more effectively what, for example, it is that determines the percentage of through traffic, I would argue that a two variable analysis as depicted on a graph or calculated by regression analysis is not enough. In fact even there variable analysis can actually prove misleading. This is especially so if we are going to be using these analyses to predict what is likely to happen in the future.

This problem is found in the whole set of interrelationships between transport, demand for land, the location decisions of industry and of population and so on. These relationships are often subsumed in any relationship which is evaluated as between transport and land use for example. In the past we have not only made very little attempt to separate out cause and effect in the actual relationships observed here; also we have failed to identify the actual relationships. In econometrics we have the statistical means of solving some of these problems of simultaneity of relationship but only after the conceptual difficulties of identifying the variables and relationships have been solved.

I would just like to extend these points a little further on to application of cost benefit analysis. Cost benefit analysis has been another example of the rather partial and narrow use of what available techniques there are. Cost benefit analyses are used very frequently to determine whether any given investment is desirable or not. Because of the partial nature of cost benefit analysis it has tended to apply a simple approach towards interactions between transport and urban planning generally. If you look at the M1 motorway cost benefit analysis you will find a very small section entitled 'Generated Traffic'. Now it is generated traffic that is the interesting bit – certainly when we are looking at urban planning. This generated traffic represents the secondary impact of the transport improvements on land use. What is needed is a general equilibrium analysis of urban planning – a general analysis of all the interrelationships between all the elements that go to make up a town. In particular we need to pass beyond two variable or even multivariable single equations. To extend the partial approach which economists tend to indulge in and to attempt to explain all the intricates i.e. we need to construct explanations so that we understand what is going on rather than just describe the situation.

R. White. It seems that there are motives in the choice of method of transport and the choice of route which cannot be quantified by other than perhaps a sociologist. This may be achieved by asking people why they adopt a certain choice and then observing that so many per cent do this and so many per cent do that. I am always suspicious of asking people in matters of this sort. I do not think we get honest answers. In the Newcastle survey it was found that no one would admit to travelling by bus because it was cheaper. There was an immediate reaction of 'Of course I can go the more expensive way', 'I am not suggesting that I cannot afford it'. This was a sort of reaction where I think people rationalize their motives and you cannot detect them by simply asking them. This is the problem. Maybe an applied psychologist could do something by some sort of simulation to find out what people's reaction is to this sense of time on a journey.

Regarding the cost benefit analysis on highway construction, I think it is fair to say that at the moment, there are two reasons why we do cost benefit studies for urban improvement. First we use the technique because it is the only way you can persuade a Public Authority that there is any return. Secondly this enables one to determine priorities. I think that in spite of all the defects in the cost benefit studies, if you keep to the same assumptions in all studies you get some ideas of which jobs are going to give you a better return immediately, and the order in which limited resources may be spent. Even if the actual figure is wrong, the order of merit is likely to be right. It has been shown that we are so far behind our approach to highway improvement in this country that almost any improvement can be justified by just going and looking at it without cost benefit analysis; this of course will not satisfy the grant awarding body. You have to find figures for it and I think this is quite proper.

On the question of generated traffic, the M1 simply did not have a land use model built into it. There was no assessment to see what the economic changes would be that might generate more traffic except on a time basis, that was all. The Erskine Bridge study for example showed quite clearly that the presence of the bridge has a reactive effect on the siting of the new town at Erskine. It is also associated with the decision to put a petro-chemical plant on the banks of the Clyde. Without the bridge I doubt if these decisions would be made.

I have done a few hypothetical calculations of this sort. We can eliminate the complexity and the problem of generated traffic by simply assessing the current benefits that would follow if the improvement were instantaneously created. This is the basis of the recommendations that the Ministry give and I think it is what one would do.

One thing about surveys and their cost. I wonder if it is realized that with very little extra cost, a lot of valuable information could be collected by the transportation engineer when he sends out his various questionnaire forms to households, factories etc. Valuable information could be produced for economists and others for quite different purposes by adding one vital question. For instance, in the study we did in Northern Ireland we simply added one vital question, 'Would you be prepared to take students during the term time and if so how many beds can you provide?' This was a vital piece of information that was lacking and was added on to the transportation study for no extra cost whatever. There are lots of little things like this that could be done. We did this in Galloway by adding information that would help the tourist board. I think this is where we need some kind of central planning authority where all studies could be coordinated between the different disciplines – a tremendous economy achieved especially nowadays with mechanical processing.

Concluding Remarks

WREFORD WATSON

I am very pleased to make the closing statement although I regret being unable to attend all the sessions in this seminar. I should however like to say, by way of an excuse, that I had to attend another conference running at the same time. I did find that this other conference which was on Eastern Europe and the Middle East did raise quite a number of issues that were very relevant for us. The person who was speaking on the USSR for example pointed out that as late as 1930 80 per cent of the people of the USSR depended on agriculture whereas today only something like 11 per cent do and in this very short space of time the USSR has changed its whole economy, its whole emphasis on life to one that is essentially urban rather than rural. Also Professor Fisher in his talk was mentioning that more and more of the development in the developing countries is going on from the city. So it does seem that almost wherever we look we see this growth in time and this geographical spread of the urban way of life. Professor Coppock mentioned yesterday that only 4 per cent of our population is engaged in agriculture and 89 per cent of our population is really following urban pursuits. A recent study of New York State indicates only 2 per cent of the population is engaged in primary occupation of agriculture, forestry, mining and fishing and that all the rest of the population is really concerned with urban pursuits. This is 9 per cent of the population.

It is obvious then that we are in the midst of a great urban revolution and that this is urbanizing the landscape far beyond the limits of the built-up area. So I am very pleased that in this conference we have again and again stressed the fact that we are dealing not just with the city but with the way of life that spreads throughout the country. I heard an interesting point of view that the townships and counties well beyond metropolitan Toronto in Canada should charge metropolitan Toronto for all the refuse with which the people of Toronto had littered the surrounding area. He calculated that two hundred-weight of litter per head of the population (including babies) was spread into the countryside by the people of Toronto and he thought it would be a fair charge on the Toronto rates. Then a year or two ago there came a report of the extraordinary pollution that had been poured into Lake Erie by all the big cities around. We are really living in an urbanized landscape that feels the impact of the city too, almost the remotest parts.

I also feel very strongly that because of the breadth of this phenomenon and its complexity it is not possible for any one of us to attempt to study this and to feel that he can do it properly. Even although each one of us tries to understand something of what is being done in other disciplines, the problem escapes us, and I think the time has come for team work, for groups like this where several disciplines are brought together where we can work together on an inter-disciplinary front. At the same time I think it is incumbent on each one of us to try to talk and learn the ideas of the related disciplines very much more.

I feel that we need very many more case studies of individual cities to determine for example the influence of the city upon the country. In this I think this seminar has shown the need for comparative studies for comparing what goes on in Europe and America and what goes on in the western world with the Middle East and southern Asia and so on. I am sure that this is tremendously important. Too many of us are gaining our knowledge of the city from literature published in English or published in German or French – we know very little of what the Indians are writing or what the Japanese are writing unless it is translated. I think that we must try to make ourselves more aware of how Asians and Africans think about the city. I am sure this is very necessary but we must pursue them in a more disciplined way.

A great number of case studies are not yet sufficiently positive and too many of them are based on the personal observations and opinions of a person or at most a small group of people. I think that in urban studies we have got to get down to quantifying our work very much more and I think that this will help to approach the problem of scale.

There are some special things I feel we must do; we must pay more attention to the trends, to the history of urban growth and to the trends which it throws out. I do not think we must keep on seeking to remake our models, and systems.

Finally, I would very much like to put a plea in for seeking to apply these studies. I think it would be very poor for our subject if we concern ourselves too much with the history of the past, too much with the comparisons of what exists in different countries, too much with theories of trying to find some kind of general systems of towns that will fit all these theories and not enough with actually planning for the growth and redevelopment of our towns. I am sure that whatever we do we must try to make our study relevant to our country and to our towns.